The Alchemist
All for Love
Arden of Faversham
The Atheist's Tragedy
Bartholmew Fair
The Beaux' Stratagem
The Broken Heart
Bussy D'Ambois
The Changeling
A Chaste Maid in Cheapside
The Country Wife
The Critic
The Devil's Law-Case
The Double-Dealer
Dr Faustus
The Duchess of Malfi
The Dutch Courtesan
Eastward Ho!
Edward the Second
Epicoene or The Silent Woman
Every Man in His Humour
A Fair Quarrel
Gammer Gurton's Needle
An Ideal Husband
The Importance of Being Earnest
The Jew of Malta
The Knight of the Burning Pestle
Lady Windermere's Fan
London Assurance
Love for Love
The Malcontent
The Man of Mode

Marriage A-la-Mode
A New Way to Pay Old Debts
The Old Wife's Tale
The Plain Dealer
The Playboy of the Western World
The Provoked Wife
The Recruiting Officer
The Relapse
The Revenger's Tragedy
The Rivals
The Roaring Girl
The Rover
The School for Scandal
She Stoops to Conquer
The Shoemaker's Holiday
The Spanish Tragedy
Tamburlaine
Three Late Medieval Morality Plays
    Mankind
    Everyman
    Mundus et Infans
Thyestes
'Tis Pity She's a Whore
Volpone
The Way of the World
The White Devil
The Witch
The Witch of Edmonton
A Woman Killed with Kindness
A Woman of No Importance
Women Beware Women

NEW MERMAIDS

General editor: Brian Gibbons
Professor of English Literature, University of Münster

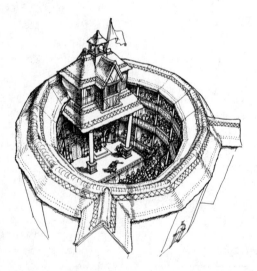

Reconstruction of an Elizabethan theatre
by C. Walter Hodges

NEW MERMAIDS

Thomas Dekker, John Ford & William Rowley

The Witch of Edmonton

edited by Arthur F. Kinney

Thomas W. Copeland Professor of Literary History
University of Massachusetts, Amherst

A & C Black • London
WW Norton • New York

First New Mermaid edition 1998
Published by A&C Black (Publishers) Limited
35 Bedford Row, London WC1R 4JH
ISBN 0-7136-4253-X

© 1998 A&C Black (Publishers) Limited

Published in the United States of America
by W.W. Norton & Company, Inc.
500 Fifth Avenue, New York, NY 10110
ISBN 0-393-90087-8

CIP catalogue records for this book are available
from the British Library and the Library of
Congress

Typeset in 9.5 on 10 pt Sabon by
Fakenham Photosetting Ltd, Fakenham, Norfolk
Printed and bound in Great Britain by
Whitstable Litho Printers Ltd,
Whitstable, Kent

CONTENTS

FOR
Roy Kendall
with gratitude

and to
Roy, Katina, Thomas and Laurence Kendall
with love

ACKNOWLEDGEMENTS

The Witch of Edmonton is a memorable, revealing and much undervalued play of the English Renaissance stage, and I am indebted to Brian Gibbons for asking me to edit it for this series, and for his many suggestions along the way. Any editor also owes a considerable debt to those who preceded him; in my case, these must include Peter Corbin, Jacqui Russell, Douglas Sedge and Simon Trussler. I was also aided by Michael Meredith, College Librarian, and Lucy Martins of Eton College; Marion J. Pringle, Librarian of the Shakespeare Birthplace Trust; Christopher Robinson, Keeper of the University of Bristol Theatre Collection; and Stephen Parks of the Beinecke Library, Librarian of the Yale University's Elizabethan Club; as well as the staffs of the British Library, the Bodleian Library, the Library of the Victoria and Albert Museum, the Houghton Library of Harvard University, the Furness Library of the University of Pennsylvania, the Henry E. Huntington Library and the Folger Shakespeare Library.

My commentary has been enriched by the counsel and suggestions of Rebecca Bushnell, Viviana Comensoli, Roy Kendall, Andrew McNeillie, Lena Cowen Orlin, Barbara Rosen, Dan Traister and Georgianna Zeigler, and I am grateful as well for the hospitality of Mary Selway. Finally, I am indebted to Kirby Farrell and to the staffs of the Massachusetts Center for Renaissance Studies and *English Literary Renaissance* for allowing me the time away to pursue this enjoyable task: Francisco Borge, Walter Chmielewski, James Dutcher, Barclay Green, R. Morgan Griffin, David Swain and Rebecca Totaro.

ARTHUR F. KINNEY

INTRODUCTION

The Authors

The title-page of the only extant early text of *The Witch of Edmonton* – the quarto of 1658 – notes that the play is 'A known true STORY. Composed into A TRAGI-COMEDY By divers well-esteemed Poets; *William Rowley, Thomas Dekker, John Ford,* &c', and these three well-known playwrights have traditionally been credited with the entire work. Of the three, the oldest and best known was Thomas Dekker. He was born in London around 1570, although nothing is known of his parents or his early life. Records show, however, that from 1598 until 1602 he was one of many playwrights hired by Philip Henslowe to write plays for his company, the Lord Admiral's Men, and it is thought that alone or in collaboration Dekker worked on some 45 plays during this period.

Dekker's earliest surviving play, *Old Fortunatus* (1599), derived from a folktale of an old beggar and his sons, establishes some of the characteristics of his work: an interest in common people, the use of traditional or contemporary material for his plots, and an unwavering concern and sympathy for the poor and the oppressed. His best and his best-known play, *The Shoemaker's Holiday*, also written in 1599, illustrates some of these same concerns, drawing on a contemporary fiction by Thomas Deloney, *The Gentle Craft*, which purports to be an historical account of shoemaking and of one shoemaker in particular, Simon Eyre, who rose to become Lord Mayor of London and to institute the annual pancake breakfast at Shrovetide. *Satiromastix* (1601), written in collaboration with John Marston, also began as a romantic comedy, but soon turned into a satirical response to Ben Jonson's *The Poetaster* of that same year, and soon constituted part of the 'war of the theatres' between those writing for adult companies and those employed by the children's companies.

The following year he struck out on his own, writing both pamphlets and plays with mixed success; often his life was difficult and impoverished. *The Wonderful Year* (1603) describes the London plague of 1602 alongside the death of Elizabeth I; the ironic title raises questions about destiny also raised in *The Witch of Edmonton*. He collaborated with Thomas Middleton in 1604–5 on two more cynical comedies of London life, *Westward Ho!* and *Northward Ho!*, doubtless capitalizing on the arrest of Jonson, George Chapman and John Marston for their alleged satire of Scots in *Eastward Ho!* (1604). During this period, Dekker also wrote *The*

Honest Whore Part I with Middleton, following it with his own *Part II* in which a prostitute becomes an honest wife, foreshadowing Winifred in *The Witch of Edmonton*. His pamphlet on *The Seven Deadly Sins of London* (1606) sympathizes with forced marriages and the fate of the bride who 'goes to church to be married, as if she went to be buried', anticipating Susan in *The Witch of Edmonton*; two other pamphlets about underworld activity in London, *The Bellman of London* and *Lantern and Candle-Light*, were published in 1608 as well as another play with Middleton, *The Roaring Girl*, romanticizing the life of Mary Frith, or Moll Cutpurse, a real-life London character alluded to in *The Witch of Edmonton* and allowing another perspective on life at the edge. A prose satire, *The Gull's Horn Book* (1609), pretends to give advice to the pompous gallant and recounts, among other matters, how a gallant behaves at the theatre. This comic work shows that Dekker had little sympathy for social pretence, a concern that is taken up more tragically with Old Carter in *The Witch of Edmonton*, as well as with Old Thorney and Young Frank.

Dekker's hand-to-mouth existence was halted when he was arrested for debt and jailed in King's Bench Prison from 1613 to 1619. Once he was released, he seemed to turn once more to the theatre. In 1620 he wrote *The Virgin Martyr* with Philip Massinger; in 1621 he collaborated on *The Witch of Edmonton*; six more plays followed, the last one extant, *London's Tempe*, performed on 29 October 1629. Dekker was buried on 25 August 1632 at St James's, Clerkenwell. Of his large body of dramatic work, only 24 plays are still extant.

John Ford was both poet and playwright; although he wrote fewer plays than Dekker, he seems to have had an easier life. He was baptized in Islington, Devon, on 17 April 1586, about 16 years younger than Dekker and about a year younger than Rowley. It is not clear if he is the John Ford who entered Exeter College, Oxford, in 1601, but it is known that he was admitted to Middle Temple, London, to study law in 1602. He left Middle Temple in 1605, having been expelled for two of those years for debt. Between 1605 and 1621 he wrote a number of poems, including *Fame's Memorial*, an elegy for the Earl of Derbyshire; *Honour Triumphant*, a 'debate' poem in dialogue among young men of fashion; and *A Line of Life*. His first known play is *The Witch of Edmonton* which clearly influenced his later drama. *Perkin Warbeck* (about 1622) also deals with a real-life character whose quiet dignity is similar to that of Winifred in the earlier play; *The Lover's Melancholy* (1628), *The Broken Heart* (1629), *'Tis Pity She's a Whore* (?1631) and *Love's Sacrifice* (1632) deal with the psychology of melancholy and madness, arranged marriage and incest. All of these plays share with *The Witch of Edmonton* a concern with moral degeneracy and self-reflection and the ordeal of self-punishment. A slighter play, a romantic comedy entitled *The Lady's Trial* (1638), is his last known work; in all, eleven of his plays survive. It is thought that Ford retired, perhaps to Devon, and died sometime around 1640.

William Rowley was born around 1585. His first recorded acting is in 1607, the same year his first two plays – *Fortune by Land and Sea* with Thomas Heywood and *The Travels of the Three English Brothers* with John Day and George Wilkins – were produced. From 1609 to 1621 he was a member of the Duke of York's Men (later Prince Charles's Men), usually taking the part of the clown. He began collaborating with Thomas Middleton on several important plays in 1617, writing the subplot of *A Fair Quarrel*; two years later he played the clown in Middleton's *The Inner Temple Masque*. That same year – 1619 – he wrote his only extant play without collaboration, *All's Lost by Lust*, a tragic melodrama which establishes the same tone as *The Witch of Edmonton* two years later with a situation similar to that of Frank Thorney. In 1622 he again returned to comedy but this time tinged with madness when writing the subplot of *The Changeling*, once more in collaboration with Middleton. In 1623 he joined the King's Men, offending the Spanish ambassador while playing the part of the fat bishop in Middleton's *A Game at Chess* (1624) and probably collaborating once more with Middleton on *The Spanish Gipsy*. In 1625 he worked with John Webster on the comedy *A Cure for a Cuckold* with the well-known clown Compass and wrote his own city comedy entitled *A Woman Never Vexed*. Rowley died in February 1626; only 16 plays have survived of more than 50 on which he worked during his lifetime.

The Play

Collaboration and Date

The well-known yet distinctive characteristics of each of the authors of *The Witch of Edmonton* have traditionally identified for critics the contribution of each to this collaborative effort. Throughout his life, Dekker's chief interest was in the functioning of society, the need for community and appeals for social concern and change. The situation faced by the real-life Elizabeth Sawyer would have attracted his deepest sympathies, but so would Frank Thorney's arranged marriage and the causes and consequences of his unintended bigamy. Sir Arthur Clarington's exploitation of Winifred and Young Frank's unintended exploitation of Susan, as well as his embarrassment before his father, are other social situations that would appeal to Dekker's deepest instincts, and it is likely that he contributed to the plot and characterization of all of these. But the heartiness of Old Carter seems particularly related to other creations of Dekker – that of Simon Eyre in *The Shoemaker's Holiday* and Orlando Frescobaldo in *The Honest Whore Part II*. Dekker's long experience in the theatre doubtless taught him much about the construction of a play, too, and he probably assigned parts of the collaboration after sensing the inherent parallels in the situations of Frank Thorney and Elizabeth (Mother) Sawyer. His interest in community suggests that he was the principal author of the scenes that bring the plots together in communal practices: the morris dance (III.i,iv) and the double execution (V.iii).

As a collaborator in what is probably his first play, John Ford would have apprenticed to the older Dekker. If this was the case, then Dekker gave to Ford situations that employed his particular talents as well. The rich psychological portrayal of Frank with Winifred, with his father and with Susan (especially in III.ii,iii) and Frank's bewildered sense of guilt before Winifred and Kate (IV.ii) display the same abilities that are later developed alone in his treatment of arranged marriage in *The Broken Heart*, death in *Love's Melancholy* and the pain of guilt-torn conscience in *'Tis Pity She's a Whore*. These later works share with *The Witch of Edmonton* a deep understanding of the complexity of attitudes of those who must live in a regulated and often repressive society.

In many ways, the story of Cuddy Banks (often referred to as Young Banks in the play) follows the traditional plot of farce, by which a clown through his love for the unavailable Kate and his credulity before the promises of Dog ends up in a prat-fall into the mud of the Edmonton marsh. Rowley would have had much experience with such lines of development, but his portrayal of clowns through the years doubtless tempered the writing of Cuddy's part, combining the clown's eagerness to have the central role – here Cuddy's desire to play the hobby-horse – with the sweetness of a simple nature, seen in his compassion for both Mother Sawyer and her familiar. Cuddy's loyalty to both enriches what might have been a limited and stereotypical part, working in tandem with the issues of loyalty raised by Dekker and Ford elsewhere in the play.

This successful orchestration of talents led in 1624 to a second collaboration for the three playwrights. Like *The Witch of Edmonton*, *The Late Murder of the Son upon the Mother*, performed in September of that year at the Red Bull but now lost, is based on current scandal. Once again two authentic incidents – the murder by Nathaniel Tindall of his mother on 9 April in Whitechapel and the marriage of Tobias Audley to the wealthy widow Anne Elsdon while she was intoxicated on 23 July – are brought together when one is tried for murder and the other for felony at the same gaol on 3 September. Dekker and Rowley were later cited for examination in Star Chamber when Anne's relatives alleged conspiracy to defame her. Dekker and Ford continued their collaboration on four plays: *The Welsh Ambassador* (1623), *The*

Sun's Darling (1624), and two plays now lost, *The Fairy Knight* and *The Bristow Merchant* (both 1624).

The Witch of Edmonton was written sometime during the summer and autumn of 1621. It follows closely Henry Goodcole's account of the execution of Elizabeth Sawyer for witchcraft on 19 April of that year, published a few days later, and a court perform-ance is recorded later that year, on 29 December during the Christmas revels. There may have been one or more performances earlier at the Cockpit Theatre in London. The same year Edward Fairfax wrote his account entitled *Daemonologie* about the bewitchment of his children, and another play, *The Merry Devil of Edmonton*, was popular in the repertoire of the King's Men. Perhaps the play was too pointedly factual for comfort, for it was not printed until 1658.

Sources and Background

The title of *The Witch of Edmonton* suggests that the chief inspi-ration of the play was the trial and execution in April 1621 of Elizabeth Sawyer on accusations of witchcraft and on an account published days later from which passages are taken verbatim for the play: '*The wonderfull discouerie of* ELIZABETH SAWYER *a Witch, late of* Edmonton, *her* conuiction and condemnation and Death. *Together with the relation of the Diuels* accesse to her, and their conference together.' According to the title-page, this work was 'Written by HENRY GOODCOLE Minister of the Word of God, and her continuall Visiter in the Gaole of Newgate' and was '*Published by Authority*' for the bookseller William Butler to be sold at his shop in St Dunstan's Churchyard in Fleet Street.

According to Goodcole, 'On Saturday, being the fourteenth day of Aprill, *Anno Dom.* 1621. this *Elizabeth Sawyer* late of *Edmonton*, in the County of *Middlesex* Spinster, was arraigned, and indited three seuerall times at Iustice Hall in the Old Baily in *London*, in the Parish of Saint *Sepulcher*, in the Ward of Farrington without: which Inditements were, *viz.* That shee the said *Elizabeth Sawyer*, not hauing the feare of God before her eyes, but moued and seduced by the Diuell, by Diabolicall helpe, did out of her malicious heart, (because her neighbours where she dwelt, would not buy Broomes of her) would therefore thus reuenge her selfe on them in this manner, namely, witch to death their Nurse Children and Cattell. ... She was also indited, for that shee the said *Elizabeth Sawyer*, by Diabolicall helpe, and out of her malice afore-thought, did witch vnto death *Agnes Ratcleife*, a neighbour of hers, ... because that *Elizabeth Ratcliefe* [sic] did strike a Sowe of hers in her sight, for licking vp a little Soape where shee had laide it, and for that *Elizabeth Sawyer* would be reuenged' (sigs. B1v–B2). Goodcole purports to recount the facts of Mother Sawyer's trial and of her

The wonderfull dis-
couerie of ELIZABETH SAVVYER
a Witch, late of Edmonton, her
conuiction and condemnation
and Death.

Together with the relation of the Diuels
accesse to her, and their conference together.

Written by HENRY GOODCOLE Minister of the
Word of God, and her continuall Visiter in the
Gaole of Newgate.

Published by Authority.

London, Printed for VVilliam Butler, and are to be sold at his Shop in Saint
Dunstons Church-yard, Fleetstreet, 1621.

Title page from 1621 edition, shelfmark C27b38, reproduced
by permission of the British Library

subsequent confession as well as to report 'what shee said at the *place of Execution*' (sigs. D2v–D3). Goodcole's portrayal is harsher than that of the playwrights, for he notes that rather than being a lonely and friendless spinster, Mother Sawyer had a husband and children and had been in communion with the Devil for a period of eight years (sig. C2v).

But for all this Goodcole wishes to appear sympathetic. In an apology to his '*Christian Readers*' (sigs. A3–A3v), he claims that

> THe Publication of this subiect whereof now I write, hath bin by importunitie extorted from me, who would haue beene content to haue concealed it, knowing the diuersitie of opinions concerning things of this nature, and that not among the ignorant, but among some of the learned. For my part I meddle hearewith nothing but matter of fact, and to that ende produce the Testimony of the liuing and the dead, which I hope shall be Authenticall for the confirmation of this Narration, and free mee from all censorious mindes and mouthes. It is none of my intent here to discuss, or dispute of Witches or Witchcraft, but desire most therin to be dispensed with all, know-ing, that in such a little Treatise as this is, no matter that can be effec-tuall therein can be comprised; especially, in so short a time of deliberation, as three or four dayes. And the rather doe I now pub-lish this to purchase my peace, which without it being done, I could scarse at any time be at quiet, for many who would take no nay, but still desired of me written Copies of this insuing Declaration. Another reason was to defend the truth of the cause, which in some measure, hath receiued a wound already, by most base and false Ballets, which were sung at the time of our returning from the Witches execution. In them I was ashamed to see and heare such ridiculous fictions of her bewitching Corne on the ground, of a Ferret and an Owle dayly sporting before her, of the bewitched woman brayning her selfe, of the Spirits attending in the Prison: all which I knew to be fitter for an Ale-bench then for a relation of proceeding in Court of Iustice. And thereupon I wonder that such lewde Balletmongers should be suffered to creepe into the Printers presses and peoples eares

As the chaplain who heard her confession, Goodcole wishes to pro-vide a full and accurate record of Mother Sawyer's life and trial as he understands it from the evidence presented in court, where he was faithful in his attendance, augmented by the words of her con-fession to him and at the block at Tyburn. As chaplain, moreover, he wishes to present her case as exemplary, and he concludes his work with an admonition to all Christians to learn from Mother Sawyer's ill-fated career how to 'Stand on your guard' against 'the Diuell your aduersary' (sig. D3).

'Elizabeth Sawyer's interrogation by her confessor,' Diane

Purkiss writes, 'is not an act of unfeeling cruelty but a way of encouraging her to utter the stories that can return her to the Christian community from which her diabolic pact had exiled her.' If so, by improving her story she may be encouraged to invent parts of it. Purkiss may also be suggesting this when she comments further that 'the confession extorted' has 'absolute spiritual value rather than legal validity', adding that 'His interest in this truth is not altogether disinterested'.[1] Indeed, Goodcole's very interests may lead to further speculation. Unable to attend the university or to gain preferment in the church until late in his life, Goodcole augmented his living by hearing confessions of those condemned at Newgate Prison and then, only a few days later, selling their stories, presumably for purposes of moral uplift and instruction.

Although many of his works may no longer be extant, two earlier pamphlets show that the account of Elizabeth Sawyer was for Goodcole only one in a series. In 1618 he had published '*A True Declaration of the happy Conuersion, contrition, and Christian preparation of FRANCIS ROBINSON, Gentleman. Who FOR COVNTERFETting the Great Seale of England, was drawen, Hang'd, and quartered at* Charing Crosse, *on Friday last, being the Thirteenth day of* Nouember' in which he proposed that 'DYing mens wordes are euer remarkable, & their last deeds memorable for succeeding posterities, by them to be instructed, what vertues or vices they followed and imbraced, and by them to learne to imitate that which was good, and to eschew euill' (sig. A4). 'LONDONS CRY' in 1620 swiftly recited the stories of such 'Bloodshedders, Burglaiers, and Vagabounds' as Andrew Ward, Thomas Horsey, Richard Harper, Thomas Porter, Samuel Prat and John Smith, all tried in late December 1619 and 'executed at Tiburne and about London'.

The success of the report on Elizabeth Sawyer may also have occasioned still a fourth work in 1637, this time exclusively about women. '*Natures Cruell She-Dames:* Or, *Matchlesse Monsters of the Female Sex;* Elizabeth Barnes, *and* Anne Willis *Who were executed the 26. day of* April, *1637 at* Tyburne, *for the unnaturall murthering of their owne Children*' is augmented by the confessions of Joan Burs and Anne Holden and the punishment of 'one Notorious Bawd *Rebecca Smith*' (sig. C3v). None of these other works displays much sympathy for the convicted and the condemned, however, and it is hard not to see Goodcole as effectually capitalizing on their misfortunes.

Goodcole's general practice of exploiting the faults of others, therefore, may have inspired Dekker and Ford to retell the story of Mother Sawyer just as much as the notoriety of her case. But they

---

[1] Typescript of 'Testimony and Truth: *The Witch of Edmonton* and *The Witches of Lancashire*' delivered by Diane Purkiss at a conference at the University of Reading in the summer of 1995 and shared with the editor

may also have themselves exploited a popular play called *The Merry Devil of Edmonton* by T. B. which one editor in 1942 has reassigned to Dekker.[2] This work is first mentioned in 1604 in *The Black Book*, apparently by then being performed by the Chamberlain's Company; it was printed in 1608, issued in a second edition in 1613 and in a third in 1617. The play's popularity may also be attested to by reference to it – in such works as Thomas Middleton's *A Mad World, My Masters* in 1608 (V.ii.108–11) and in the Prologue to Jonson's *The Devil Is an Ass*, written about 1616 and performed by the King's Men at Blackfriars that autumn. There were at least two royal performances, in 1613 at Whitehall and in 1618 before the King. It is in this play that the authors of *The Witch of Edmonton*, with their already intimate knowledge of greater London, with its Paris Garden and its Thieving Lane, could augment their information with such place-names around Edmonton as Waltham, Waltham Abbey, Waltham Forest, Enfield Chase and Cheshunt (Cheston; Chesson).

While the genial devil of the earlier play, Peter Fabell, bears no resemblance to Mother Sawyer, the overplots of both plays share certain similarities. Sir Arthur Clare – whose name may have suggested that for the fictitious Sir Arthur Clarington – in collusion with his wife in *The Merry Devil of Edmonton* interrupts the betrothal of his daughter Millicent to the knight Mounchensey for 'the lusty heire of Sir Ralph Ierningham' (I.i.97–8; sig. B1v) named Frank, just as Old Carter in *The Witch of Edmonton* breaks off the betrothal of his daughter Susan to Warbeck for the more promising match with the equally fictional *Frank* Thorney. The similarity is made clearer in a soliloquy by Fabell, although the new arrangements are for money, not social advancement as in the case of the impecunious Thorneys.

> Good old Mounchensey, is thy hap so ill,
> That for thy bounty and thy royall parts
> Thy kind alliance should be held in scorne,
> And after all these promises by Clare
> Refuse to giue his daughter to thy sonne,
> Onely because thy Reuenues cannot reach
> To make her dowage of so rich a ioynture
> As can the heire of wealthy Ierningham?
> And therefore is the false foxe now in hand
> To strike a match betwixt her and th'other;
> And the old gray-beards now are close together,
> Plotting it in the garden

(I.iii.1–12; sigs. B2v–B3)

[2] William Amos Abrams, ed., *The Merry Devil of Edmonton* (Durham, North Carolina, 1942), pp. 72–103

Like Frank Thorney, however, Frank Ierningham has a previous love in distant Essex:

> With my vaine breath I will not seeke to slubber
> Her angell like perfections; but thou know'st
> That Essex hath the Saint that I adore ...
> I will abiure both beauty and her sight,
> And will in loue become a counterfeit
>
> (I.iii.82–84, 100–1; sigs. B3v–B4)

The overplot of *The Witch of Edmonton*, then, may have found its beginning in the overplot of the earlier play, just as the miller *Banks*, whose poaching of venison gets him wet, may have provided allusions to *The Merry Devil of Edmonton* in the underplot as well. This play, and the pamphlets of Henry Goodcole, together seem to have awakened the individual talents of Dekker, Ford and Rowley noted above.

Theme and Structure

For W. A. Neilson *The Witch of Edmonton* is 'a domestic tragedy of great impressiveness';[3] for Clifford Leech, 'It is a remarkable play, perhaps the best in which Dekker was ever concerned.'[4] Yet for all the emphasis on domestic relationships in the overplot with the Thorneys, the Carters, Warbeck, Somerton, and even Sir Arthur Clarington, the play always stresses interpersonal and familial relationships as part of a larger community. The play is essentially about village life, about the sacredness of the community and about the dangers inherent in any threats to its ability to integrate successfully all of its members. In this play, the community of Edmonton maintains its integrity and solidarity by keeping out destructive forces and by reducing dissension within its boundaries by shared laws and customs. The widely felt reliance on harmony, fostered in the morris dance and, more negatively, preserved in the double executions of Frank and Mother Sawyer, depends on the community's ability to identify, expose and punish any threat to the status quo; but the playwrights also keenly observe that the other side of the communal coin is the stratification and regimentation of class and gender that allow a community to continue to function without change.

Preserving the community comes at the cost of individuality. This is reflected structurally when two unconventional opening attitudes – the unexpected sympathy for the witch Mother Sawyer and the

---

[3] Quoted in *Cambridge History of English Literature* (Cambridge, 1910), VI, Part 2, p. 190

[4] Clifford Leech, *John Ford and the Drama of his Time* (London, 1957), pp. 26–7

naming of the play for the underplot rather than the overplot – are, by the play's conclusion, reassigned a familiar conventionality. At the end of *The Witch of Edmonton*, both the underplot and overplot merge in the punishments of the two characters who seem most to challenge its authority. Like the distich which stands guard at the opening of the playtext, the two parallel plots in which Frank Thorney and Mother Sawyer are tempted to determine their own fates are fused into one, and their deaths restore the community of Edmonton, if in an uneasy way. Although saddened by events, Old Carter invites everyone to join him 'merry as we can, though not as we would'; the Justice urges them to 'make of all the best'; and Winifred pledges that she will never again 'swerve / From modest hopes'. As the title-page proclaims, *The Witch of Edmonton* attempts to be both a tragedy and a comedy, like so many plays of its time.

Inevitability seems to control events, so that Frank can note that 'No man can hide his shame from Heaven that views him. / In vain he flees, whose destiny pursues him'. This observation is correct, and is reinforced by the prescriptive proverbs that Old Carter (and later Kate) speak, and the prophecies and spells that Mother Sawyer and Dog pronounce through intuition and charms. Yet, in their accumulation, these proverbs and prophecies seem somehow profoundly to *mis*represent this play. For at an even deeper level, *The Witch of Edmonton* is irrevocably troubling. The events and the characters have the power to disturb readers and spectators. Events – from Frank's bigamy to Mother Sawyer's observance of a maddened Anne Ratcliffe to Cuddy Banks' betrayal by Dog – rupture intentions. Good characters fall relatively easy prey to temptations and even the foolish come to harm others.

Starting with the illicit sexual activities of Sir Arthur Clarington, nothing in the play is quite what it first seems and the vaunted power of the community seems helpless before unsettling events. The two chief attempts to restore harmony point directly to this incongruity: the morris dance is invaded by Dog who strips Sawgut the fiddler from his sweet music and ends the dance in chaos; the execution leaves those who remain feeling sad and somehow helpless. Just as the forces on which community is based are unable to prevent the breaking of custom, so the forces of punishment are unable to heal. *The Witch of Edmonton* may derive its name not so much from the underplot as to indicate that the play is really about what may fracture community. In this sense, the witch stands for all the destructive forces in the play and allows something else which pervades it – a sense of yearning for something more, something else. Just as Frank wants Winifred, so Old Thorney needs an alliance with Old Carter; just as Mother Sawyer needs to steal sticks to keep warm, so Cuddy yearns for Kate. Frank may provide the audience with an even deeper awareness of the play's significance when he remarks, 'All life is but a wandering to find home.'

This is not to say that the play is subversive, but that its honesty
in anatomizing community life in early modern England is as precise and insightful as the attempt to get the facts and wording right
(with the help of Henry Goodcole) in relaying the testimony of
Mother Sawyer. The playwrights take their journalistic representations of events, activities and characters seriously. And in doing so,
they are especially keen on showing how the forces of society work.

It has long been noted that beginning with II.i the portrayal of
Mother Sawyer is one of social construction – that is, an examination of the ways in which a culture's values and practices dictate
the beliefs and behaviour of its members, shape their expectations
and very lives, and ensure a kind of prejudgment that erases any
possibility for individual awareness and growth. Elizabeth Sawyer
makes it clear that she is not initially a witch and that Old Banks in
calling her one leans too heavily on her appearance and her poverty.
The authors show that Mother Sawyer takes up the cultural practices of witchcraft because she feels she has no choice. Her community has already branded her a witch whether she is or not. So
she may as well be one. Cursing her misfortune, she allows an agent
of the Devil to appear, and his promise to better her conditions
when no other agent will is the sufficient cause for defeating her
once-proud spirit. In its very simplicity and commonness, this
sequence of events is deeply troubling, and highly tragic. Moreover,
it overturns all that Henry Goodcole reports about Mother
Sawyer's crime and seriously interrogates the wisdom of his
pamphlet.

But the playwrights are not content to stop with this dreadful
social construction of Mother Sawyer. One of the basic purposes of
the double plot, and of the play, is to show that her situation is
essentially no different from Frank's. In his case, moreover, social
conditioning and social construction work in a double way that
puts him in a double bind. The social custom of enforced marriages,
or marriages by arrangement, which the class structure found vital
to sustain itself (as Old Thorney feels he must preserve his fortune
and his class even by marrying his son off to the daughter of a
wealthy yeoman who is socially beneath him), corners Frank in a
desperate choice between bigamy and disobedience, a dilemma in
which he cannot win. Either way – admitting his earlier marriage to
a servant girl; denying his father – he loses; and in the second situation, as Old Thorney makes clear, he loses both their fortunes,
both his father's security and his own legacy. This would be bad
enough, but Frank faces a social construction of morality and guilt
that counters his surrender to marry Susan with an unimpeachable
and insistent sense of irresponsibility to Winifred and deep personal
guilt. Both society and morality work against him. Yet, on reflection, the same double bind is also true of Mother Sawyer. In choosing to behave like a witch, she must become one: having called up

Dog with her cursing, she is threatened with bodily dismemberment if she does not bend totally to his will.

Like Frank, then, Mother Sawyer is forced suddenly to face her own moral shortcomings and miscalculations and, like Frank, she has no one to console her. The individuality of her situation is accompanied, like his, with a kind of unbearable solitude and isolation. Her struggle to free herself from the overbearing presence of Dog is made deliberately parallel to Frank's inability to free himself from Susan's presence, and the results are equally tragic: Mother Sawyer's powers are blamed for Anne Ratcliffe's madness and suicide, as Frank's own entrapment forces him to murder Susan. Although both initially deny such charges, society ignores them – rightly, in the case of Frank – and, finding them wrongdoers, eliminates them from the society forever with capital punishment.

On the face of it, few issues might seem more distant than witchcraft and enforced marriage – the first the subject of Thomas Middleton's play *The Witch* (1610), the second the subject of George Wilkins' domestic tragicomedy *The Miseries of Enforced Marriage* (1607). A large number of plays and treatises on enforced marriage were published in England between 1600 and 1650 just as there were a number of witchcraft plays and pamphlets; both themes have in common social situations that emerge from an increase in the inequality of wealth and social status. Just as poverty drives Mother Sawyer, so the threat of poverty drives Old Thorney and, in turn, his son.

That the force of a class structure and the dangers of inequality are important to this play is made clear in Act I when we learn that Sir Arthur Clarington, who at first appears sympathetic to Frank and Winifred, is actually using them to his own ends; his striking lack of humanity in his treatment of them anticipates Old Banks' lack of humaneness with Mother Sawyer. The physical beating of Mother Sawyer at the hands of Old Banks only externalizes the more subtle beating of young Frank by his conspiratorial father and, more subtly yet, the abuse of Winifred at the hands of Sir Arthur. The play thus encourages its audience to see criminals as often victims of forces and situations not of their own making nor even of their own choosing. Rather, they are caught in a society in which what they yearn for is not ever realizable.

It is in just this way that the comic relief provided by the story of Cuddy Banks highlights the other two plots, for Cuddy is also severely limited in his pursuit of Kate Carter by his own class. Although it may not be apparent at first, Old Banks never appears in any scenes with a Clarington, a Thorney or a Carter; he is even absent from the morris dance held at Sir Arthur's house. While Cuddy is allowed to be there – though only as entertainment, not as a guest – his own benefit is to find someone he can love but cannot marry, cannot even address except as a spirit induced by Dog, in one of the play's meaner tricks. Rather, Old Banks is allowed conversation only with Mother Sawyer and his son. Even at the end of the play, when it would appear the entire community assembles to see the executions of Frank and Mother Sawyer, neither Old Banks nor Cuddy – nor any of their fellow morris dancers and musicians – is allowed to be present.

Cuddy Banks may appear foolish at that morris dance, for he appears as the animal, the hobby-horse who, unlike his fellows, is partly covered in a disguise; he may also appear foolish in his chase after the false Duessa of a Kate, ending in a fall into the Edmonton marsh, but expressed by both the chief events in this strand of plot is a similar frustration that, in other registers, also characterizes not only Frank and Mother Sawyer, but Winifred and Susan too. Although Cuddy does not participate in illegal contracts of bigamy or witchcraft, he nevertheless contracts himself to his desire for Kate and winds up, as they do, painfully aware of the restrictions that control him in Edmonton. Only the one non-citizen, Dog, seems to have power and liberty to do what he wants – to rub his victims and thus gain joy. While Dog alone moves through all three strands of the play, however, he too is subject to the powers of evil, unable to do good. The most he can do, as he makes clear to Cuddy, is to withhold evil; he cannot perform good. The range of his possibilities too is limited, and his freedom a delusion. Just as Cuddy exposes Dog's own limitations to him, so the playwrights, throughout *The Witch of Edmonton*, expose the limitations of a rural early modern English village which is organized by class and privilege and whose activity, therefore, fosters intrigue and deception.

The negotiations of Sir Arthur and Winifred and of Winifred and Frank in I.i are not mocked so much as paralleled by the negotiations of Old Carter and Old Thorney and of Old Thorney and his son in I.ii while in Act II Mother Sawyer's deprivation – the meagre sticks which will keep her warm – is replayed in Act III in Cuddy's deprivation of Kate – the dream he can never possess. The community of Edmonton, then, is tested by – and calls forth sympathy for – its outcasts, victims and scapegoats; in Edmonton, it would seem, nearly everyone is guilty of something and that something, more often than not, is a self-interest that blinds them to the needs of their families and neighbours and that threatens the very community they most mean to and need to preserve. There also remains a certain cynicism at the end of the play when the most intentionally mean and selfish person of them all – Sir Arthur – escapes without any harsh punishment, pain, or even remorse. His active scheming in Act I, the morris dance at his home in Act III, and his light sentence in Act V frame the play with his haunting presence, contributing to its final, troubling atmosphere.

The conventionality of the play's language reinforces its conventional characterizations. Members of the aristocracy and gentry speak in poetry; those at the level of yeomen or beneath speak largely in prose (one notable exception is Mother Sawyer with her continually simple eloquence). Frank calls on mythology when speaking of love to Susan; Cuddy's speech is limited to a knowledge of folk ritual when talking with his fellow dancers. Despite Old Carter's attempt to elevate his station through the marriage of his daughter, his constant recourse to proverbial lore as the most apt form of wisdom marks him socially. The playwrights even use the higher-class *thou* and the lower-class *you* as signs of social status. The hierarchy of persons is guaranteed in the play by the hierarchy of their language.

Setting

Mark Kishlansky reckons that in the early part of the seventeenth century over 80 per cent of the population of England lived in the country. 'The south-east was dotted with villages rather than homesteads. The steeple was in plain view of closely built dwellings which were centred on either the churchyard or the green. Fields, meadows and commons surrounded the village and were the site of communal agricultural activities, though each family owned its own land and harvested its own crops. Kinship was comparatively weak, and the social structure of the village was determined more by wealth and standing than by blood.'[5] The agrarian economy was primarily a subsistence economy, with farmers raising their own crops, keeping a few animals and gathering what grew wild, providing all they needed to survive. Common ploughing allowed villages to keep down the cost of oxen and ploughshares; communal foddering maximized fertilization; and taxation in kind was self-regulated to surplus and shortage. 'As a mode of economic organisation, the family was the primary unit of production. Most marriages were made on economic calculations, with the timing dependent upon inheritance or the completion of apprenticeship or domestic service. Marriage contracts, especially among the wealthy, were complex prenuptial agreements that specified the dowry the woman would bring and the portion she would receive as widow.' He adds that 'prevailing wisdom held that love was an emotion acquired within marriage rather than before'.[6]

Such a straightforward, if limiting, existence helped to preserve the universality of social definition and distinction. 'It is hard,' Kishlansky continues, 'to determine whether distinctions of status were invidious. They had legal standing not only in the regulation of rights and responsibilities but also in sumptuary legislation that

---

[5] Mark Kishlansky, *A Monarchy Transformed: Britain 1603–1714* (London, 1996), pp. 6–7

[6] Kishlansky, pp. 12–13

John Speed's 1612 map of Middlesex from *The Theater of the World*, call number STC 2340, reproduced by permission of the Folger Shakespeare Library, Washington

governed what could be worn or consumed by different orders of people. Thus social distinction was constantly on display in dress, demeanour and deportment, and it was continually reinforced by deference which ranged from modes of speech and forms of address to the doffing of caps and ceding the right of way.'[7] Yeomen and husbandmen were usually the leaders of village society; called 'goodman' they outranked cottagers and labourers both by their wealth and by their social responsibilities.

Many villagers were poor. Kishlansky reports that 'A subsistence agrarian economy could expect to have over a quarter of its population chronically poor and another quarter cyclically poor.'[8] While numbers are difficult to ascertain, in at least one rural parish in Essex at this period two-thirds of the population was below or just at the poverty line. 'Abandoned wives and unmarried mothers were among the most common of the wandering poor – the wives searching for their husbands; the unmarried fleeing a life of shame.'[9] Frequently these poor were divided into the impotent and the idle, into 'God's poor and the Devil's'.

There were 600 communicants in Edmonton parish in 1547; plague claimed 85 out of 145 deaths in 1601; 53 of the 157 people buried in 1625. In the period 1571 to 1588 Elizabeth's Principal Secretary, William Cecil, Lord Burghley, owned 2000 acres of the parish. For most of its history in the sixteenth and early seventeenth century, the success of farming in the parish of Edmonton was mixed. The generally low, flat land was crossed by two tributaries of the Lea River which often made the meadowland soft and waterlogged; the marsh into which Cuddy Banks falls is representative of a region where farming could never be extremely prosperous. Instead, the land was used to pasture pigs and cattle and to support such basic crops as wheat, oats, rye, barley, peas and beans. According to maps of Edmonton drawn around 1600, the village itself about the time of *The Witch of Edmonton* consisted of roughly 182 houses clustered around Lower and Upper Edmonton with a line of smaller hamlets, such as Winchmore Hill and Southgate, between them. Edmonton was thus a comparatively large village; it supported several brewers, tailors and butchers as well as some specialized craftsmen, a print-maker and a clockmaker.

What communal life there was at Edmonton, as elsewhere, was in folk ritual and festivity such as church ales and morris dancing; at South Warnborough during Whitsun in 1611 the morris bells were lost, causing considerable consternation. In 1631 the author

---

[7] Kishlansky, p. 25
[8] Kishlansky, pp. 26–7
[9] Kishlansky, p. 28

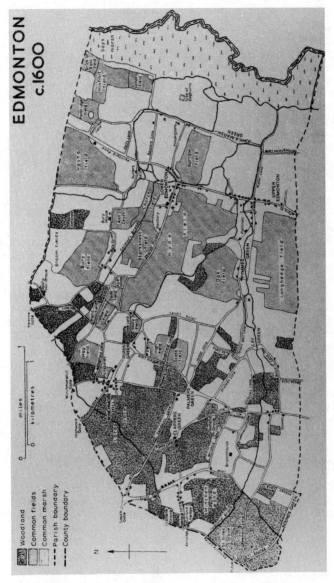

1600 map of Edmonton in *Victoria County History of Middlesex*, reproduced by permission of the Institute of Historical Research, University of London

Richard Brathwait calls 'A Countery *Rush-bearing*' a 'Morris *Pastorall*', and David George has found a 'ceremony in Whalley in 1604, which now seems representative, [that] combined rushbearing with morris dancing' and adds that 'even York and Chester injunctions suggest the practice was widespread'.[10] Parish dancing was common during Whitsun and Hocktide (celebrated on the second Monday/Tuesday after Easter) and some parishes set aside other specific 'dancing days'. Other festivities featured Robin Hood and his followers, morris dances and maypoles, and fragmentary evidence suggests that Robin Hood, as a disturber of the peace, as a figure of combat, opposed the summer lord, at first providing, and then in defeat containing, a sense of revolt or dissension. Alexandra F. Johnston has found a sixteenth-century text from Woodstock and a later one from Whitney where 'two parish troupes – Robin Hood and his company and the morris dancers possibly led by the friar figure – come together for a farce full of horseplay and violence that ends with a dance'.[11]

Antagonism such as that between Old Banks and Mother Sawyer was thus contained in the ritual that Cuddy prepares as an entertainment for Sir Arthur. Although the authors of *The Witch of Edmonton* may have been unaware of the details of the town and parish where Elizabeth Sawyer was arrested and accused of witchcraft, they may have known of the marshes and fens of Edmonton where Cuddy could probably feel the danger of drowning, and they understood fully the utility of the dance of Act III, as well as the grim significance of its dispersal due to the devilish antics of Dog.

Witchcraft

The failed morris dance in the climactic Act III of *The Witch of Edmonton* may be crucial to the playwrights' portrayal of the town. While the authors of *The Witch of Edmonton* might know little of such performances, even in Edmonton, they would be well aware of descriptions circulated in London, beginning with Phillip Stubbes' *Anatomie of Abuses … in the Country of Ailgna* as early as 1583:

> First, all the wildheads of the parish, conventing together, choose them a grand captain (of all mischief) whom they ennoble with the title of 'my Lord of Misrule', and him they crown with great solemnity, and adopt for their king. This king anointed chooseth forth

---

[10] David George, 'Rushbearing: A Forgotten British Custom' in *English Parish Drama*, eds, Alexandra F. Johnston and Win Hüsken (Amsterdam, 1996), pp. 24–5

[11] Alexandra F. Johnston, '"What Revels are in Hand?": Dramatic Activities Sponsored by the Parishes of the Thames Valley' in Johnston and Hüsken, p. 97

twenty, forty, threescore or a hundred lusty guts, like to himself, to
wait upon his lordly majesty and to guard his noble person. Then
every one of these his men, he investeth with his liveries of green,
yellow, or some other light wanton colour. And as though that were
not (bawdy) gaudy enough, I should say, they bedeck themselves
with scarves, ribbons and laces hanged all over with gold rings, pre-
cious stones, and other jewels. This done, they tie about either leg
twenty or forty bells, with rich handkerchiefs in their hands, and
sometimes laid across over their shoulders and necks, borrowed for
the most part of their pretty Mopsies and loving Besses, for bussing
them in the dark.

   Thus all things set in order, then have they their hobby-horses,
dragons and other antiques [antics?] together with their bawdy
pipers and thundering drummers to strike up the devil's dance withal.
Then march these heathen company towards church and churchyard,
their pipers piping, their drummers thundering, their stumps dancing,
their bells jingling, their handkerchiefs swinging about their heads
like madmen, their hobby-horses and other monsters skirmishing
amongst the rout. And in this sort they go to the church (I say) and
into the church (though the minister be at prayer or preaching) dancing and swinging their handkerchiefs over their heads in the church,
like devils incarnate, with such a confused noise, that no man can
hear his own voice. Then the foolish people they look, they stare,
they laugh, they fleer, and mount upon forms and pews to see these
goodly pageants solemnized in this sort.[12]

Although there is no churchyard in this play – it is instead the home
of the evil Sir Arthur – the morris dance nevertheless provides the
same natural setting for the devil, or Dog. In fact, Cuddy Banks has
already prepared the way, for he has long wanted a witch at their
festivity, thus indirectly inviting the witch's familiar to join them
and to demonize their dance.

   But then 'The land is full of witches', Lord Chief Justice Anderson
declared in 1602; 'They abound in all places'.[13] Witchcraft was even
more common in agrarian villages where unprofitable weather,
cattle and crops – the people's very livelihood – had to be explained.
Christina Larner notes that it was just those most unpredictable fea-
tures of life – 'sudden illness, certain accidents, lingering illness for
which no cause was clear, strokes, unexpected deaths, the failure of
crops, especially if other people's were doing well, the drying up of
milk, human or animal, strange behaviour in animals' – that were,

---

[12] Ed. F. J. Furnivall (London, 1877–82), pp. 147–8, as quoted in C. L. Barber,
   Shakespeare's Festive Comedy (Princeton, 1959), pp. 27–8
[13] Quoted in Keith Thomas, *Religion and the Decline of Magic* (Harmondsworth,
   1978, 1988), p. 542

systematically, assigned to witches and witchcraft.[14] There was inherent in communities like Edmonton a necessity for witches. And as in the play, 'From the initial accusation to the final judicial hearing,' Keith Thomas writes, 'the procedure followed in the witch cases reminds us at every stage that men seldom seek a high degree of proof for what they already believe to be true ... the standard of evidence required to secure a conviction for witchcraft was particularly unexacting'.[15] Furthermore, 'confessions, whether genuine or extorted, agree in suggesting that accused persons lived in a state of impotence and desperation. Their commonest motive was thought to be the desire to escape from grinding poverty'.[16]

Thomas traces the cause of such poverty to the breakdown of the old manorial system by which 'a built-in system of poor relief' had been practised by the local gentry.[17] Such gentry in *The Witch of Edmonton* are represented by Sir Arthur Clarington whose direct selfishness and exploitation of Frank and Winifred is thus indirectly extended to Mother Sawyer whose poverty forces her to steal from Old Banks: when Cuddy calls for a witch at Sir Arthur's home, then, and when Dog appears, there may be a subtle insinuation in the play that Sir Arthur is even more deeply implicated than the explicit plot-line allows.

Yet with whatever ease Old Banks and his son accuse Mother Sawyer of witchcraft, they have for the time sufficient reason. According to William Perkins in his *Discourse of the Damned Art of Witchcraft* (1608), the key factor is 'consenting to use the help of the devil, either by open or secret league, wittingly and willingly: wherein standeth the very thing that maketh a witch to be a witch, the yielding of consent upon covenant'.[18] Even though Dog threatens Mother Sawyer with physical mutilation, frightening her, the moment she allows him to suck her blood she is, by the standards of early Stuart England, eternally damned. She is from that point on liable to the statute known as 'An Act against conjuration witchcraft and dealing with evil and wicked spirits', passed in 1604 as James I, chapter 12, which established that

> if any person or persons, after the said Feast of St. Michael the Archangel next coming, shall use practise or exercise any invocation or conjuration of any evil and wicked spirit, or shall consult, covenant with, entertain, employ, feed, or reward any evil and

[14] Christina Larner, *Witchcraft and Religion: The Politics of Popular Belief* (Oxford, 1984), p. 74

[15] Thomas, p. 658

[16] Thomas, p. 621

[17] Thomas, p. 670

[18] *Works*, ed. Ian Breward (Berkshire, 1970), p. 596

wicked spirit to or for any intent or purpose ... or shall use, practise, or exercise any witchcraft, enchantment, charm, or sorcery, whereby any person shall be killed, destroyed, wasted, consumed, pined, or lamed in his or her body, or any part thereof; that then every such offender or offenders, their aiders abetters and counsellors, being of any the said offences duly and lawfully convicted and attainted, shall suffer pains of death as a felon or felons, and shall lose the privilege and benefit of clergy and sanctuary.[19]

In reviewing the events of *The Witch of Edmonton* for the *Times Literary Supplement* in 1981, R. V. Holdsworth argues that the fit of madness suffered by Anne Ratcliffe was actually an attack of epilepsy – so that Mother Sawyer is blameless in her death – and that Mother Sawyer's 'witch's teat' 'judging from the information gloatingly supplied by her interrogator, the Reverend Henry Goodcole, was actually a thrombosed pile'.[20] Today's medical knowledge, then, establishes Mother Sawyer's innocence, for even though she made a covenant with Dog, no bodily harm was caused as a result. In this sense, Mother Sawyer is less responsible for confusion and concern in Edmonton than Cuddy Banks, who brought Dog into the morris dance, and there is no legal grounds for her execution.

The playwrights show, through their social construction of Mother Sawyer, that they are well aware of her essential helplessness and innocence. In *The Witch of Edmonton*, she is meant not primarily as a case study in village concerns with witchcraft but as only the most explicit sign of what the play really centres on: unassimilable women in the community, or what Viviana Comensoli has defined in part as 'old or diseased spinsters, widows, prostitutes, obstreperous wives, healers, and midwives'.[21] Such powers extend well beyond Mother Sawyer.

The play opens with the threat of another woman – the pregnant Winifred who has the power to name the father of her child and so, in a sense, dominates both Sir Arthur and Frank. In the early Stuart years when, David Underdown proposes, there was general unrest due to overpopulation, unemployment, poverty, plague and divisions over religion and government – and when women took prominent roles in food and grain riots as in the dispute over rights to the town common of Acton in 1616 – the power of women was becom-

---

[19] As reprinted in Barbara Rosen, ed., *Witchcraft in England, 1558–1618*, 2nd edn (Amherst, 1991), pp. 57–8

[20] R. V. Holdsworth, 'Vices and Victims', *Times Literary Supplement* (25 September 1981), p. 1099

[21] Viviana Comensoli, *'Household Business': Domestic Plays of Early Modern England* (Toronto, 1996), p. 112

ing more and more evident.[22] Winifred's power thus violates the position traditional for women, to 'stay at home and look after the affairs of the household', as Luther put it,[23] as well as the traditional role of servant who should never place demands on her master. But in fact the plot crucially turns on Winifred's unusual power: by the end of the play she alone has convicted both Frank and Sir Arthur, leading to the death of one and the penalty levelled on the other. She, in fact, controls the fate of people (notably men) in the way that Mother Sawyer never does. Her ease at crossdressing as Young Frank's page, though she has no name when assuming this role, shows her potentiality for subversion, the ability for metamorphosis within her highly regulated community.

Nor is she alone. Susan Carter too exercises power; her consent to marry Frank saves Old Thorney from financial disaster and transforms Old Carter's social standing: the agent of significant change is a woman. When the force of godly conscience appears in the play – even to the point of directly opposing Dog – it comes in the shape of a woman in Susan's spirit; when the shape of temptation arises for the innocent Young Cuddy it is in the form of her sister Kate.

But Frank has long been aware of the power of women. In making his remark to Susan that 'a woman / Known and approved in palmistry' has predicted his fortune, he is referring to the kind of 'wise woman' that Thomas Heywood staged in 1604 as *The Wise Woman of Hogsdon*:

> Let me see how many trades have I to live by; first, I am a wise-woman, and a fortune-teller, and under that I deal in physic and fore-speaking, in palmistry, and recovering of things lost; next, I undertake to cure mad folks; then I keep gentlewomen lodgers, to furnish such chambers as I let out by the night; then I am provided for bringing young wenches to bed; and, for a need, you see I can play the match-maker.

Frank may have the powers of such a 'wise woman' in mind – negatively, she would be called a 'witch' – because she can predict his destiny, read his palm and engineer his marriage(s). But Heywood also makes her a charlatan:

> If any knock, you must to the door and question them, to find what they come about, – if to this purpose, or to that. Now, they ignorantly telling thee their errand, which I, sitting in my closet, overhear,

[22] David Underdown, *A Freeborn People: Politics and the Nation in Seventeenth-Century England* (Oxford, 1996), pp. 18, 60

[23] Quoted in Comensoli, p. 117

presently come forth, and tell them the cause of their coming, with every word that hath passed betwixt you in private; which they admiring, and thinking it to be miraculous, by their report I become thus famous.[24]

Frank is thus vulnerable in his credulity (as, in this conversation, Susan is too), but the deceit from which he suffers is not from women but from Sir Arthur. If his employer had taken responsibility for Winifred's pregnancy, or if his domination over her had not prevented her telling Frank herself, he would not have married her and there would be no bigamy. In this play about apparently unassimilable women, they in the end only take the blame for Sir Arthur's behaviour, behaviour that is accustomed, built into the social system and mores of Edmonton. Unassimilable women, then, are the key: they are not the theme but the means by which the authors of the play point to the inherent evils of a society unwilling to examine its own codes and behaviour.

That witchcraft itself is a means and not the subject is made clear by Mother Sawyer in her final scenes. Her apparently incoherent remark to Anne Ratcliffe that she is a lawyer may indicate that we should watch her judgments. It reminds us of what otherwise seems artificial and forced, her accusations against 'your painted things in princes' courts? / Upon whose eyelids lust sits blowing fires / To burn men's souls in sensual hot desires' and others culpable of ill behaviour in IV.i. Her remarks are, however, framed with a decisive focus on Sir Arthur. To the Justice, Mother Sawyer says, 'Men in gay clothes, / Whose backs are laden with titles and honours, / Are within far more crooked than I am; / And if I be a witch, more witch-like'; at the end she transfers the charge into punishment, usurping the powers of the Justice and the courts: 'Run at a fairer game. That foul-mouthed knight, / Scurvy Sir Arthur, fly at him, my Tommy; / And pluck out's throat'.

In an age in which the picture of a woman riding on the back of a man adorned *The Brideling, Sadling and Ryding, of a rich Churle in Hampshire* published in 1595, the real danger of empowered women was their ability not merely to rule over men but to bring about a justice – here through the accusations of Winifred and Mother Sawyer – that was lacking under their assailable rule.

Enlightenment is also disenchantment. The injustice of *The Witch of Edmonton* finally overpowers the spectacle and the fun with Cuddy Banks: the morris dance at Sir Arthur Clarington's house is displaced by executions for which he takes little responsibility. In naming their play *The Witch of Edmonton*, Dekker, Ford and Rowley clearly meant to capitalize on the sensationalism and the-

---

[24] Quoted in Rosen, p. 224

atricality of witchcraft and on the cause célèbre of the death of Elizabeth Sawyer. But in writing their play, they also transformed their anatomy of a community into an examination of the corrupt power and the need for justice that the witch, in the wider sense, brings to this dramatic analysis of a representative early modern community named Edmonton.

The Play on the Stage

The first recorded performance of *The Witch of Edmonton* was by the Prince's Men on 29 December 1621, but there were quite likely public performances at the Cockpit Theatre before and after; although the play was not printed until 1658, the title-page proclaims that the play was 'Acted by the Princes Servants, often at the Cock-pit in *Drury-Lane*, once at Court, with singular Applause'. The play was revived in the early 1630s.

There have also been many records of productions in the twentieth century. The first of these was by the Phoenix Society at the Lyric, Hammersmith, with Sybil Thorndike playing Mother Sawyer. According to the reviewer for the London *Times*, she 'acted the part with her usual nervous energy: but she made the mistake of dressing and acting the witch like something out of *Macbeth* or the Irving *Faust*, instead of taking advantage of the delightful illustration printed on the programme, and dressing and acting the part within that contemporary, tragi-comical convention which Mr. Russell Thorndike very cleverly preserved in his acting of the Devil-Dog. The best thing in the whole play, and the acting, was the Old Carter of Mr. Joseph A. Dodd the rough generous, humoursome English yeoman richly imagined.'[25] The work fared better with Edith Evans as Mother Sawyer in a London production in December 1936; on this occasion, the *Times* reviewer saw the play as 'stamped with sympathy for the outcast and suffering ... able to see always two sides of the human picture – even when the picture is of a villain or a witch. In brief, it has pity, and through all its violence, there is perceptible a warmth and gentleness of the dramatist's mind.' Here 'Mr. Marius Goring,' who played Frank, 'makes the most of this aspect of the play, and so gives life to all his scenes' and Edith Evans 'has the subtlety to discover Dekker's compassion for the witch'.[26]

A production opened at the Mermaid Theatre in May 1962. According to one review, the play was 'a fascinating rag-bag of the dramatic idioms of its time', but while Bernard Miles' production had 'its wooden moments', still 'for most of the way it is an unobtrusive instrument of the text – relaxed, intelligent, and expressive

[25] Unsigned, *The Times* (of London), 27 April 1921, p. 10
[26] Unsigned, *The Times* (of London), 9 December 1936, p. 12

– there is no rhetoric. As the murderous bigamist, Mr. William Lucas adopts a vein of low-keyed realism which comes over with brutal impact, and Timothy Bateson, in the Bottom-like part of Cuddy, plays with explosive comedy. But,' he concludes, 'it is the scenes between the old woman and her familiar, locked together in a sad mockery of passion, that struck deepest in the mind.'[27]

The prompt-book is available for the most famous of modern productions, that of the Royal Shakespeare Company which first opened at The Other Place in Stratford in September 1981. For Irving Wardle of *The Times*, this was Frank's play:

> [Mother Sawyer's story] occupies less of the action than the inter-woven tragedy of an enforced marriage between young Frank who betrays his unacknowledged first wife by marrying the daughter of a wealthy yeoman to save his father from bankruptcy.
>
> In the hands of Dekker and co. this well-worn theme blossoms into a highly developed psychological drama. The only villain is contingency. You see Frank submitting to one inescapable compromise after another and threshing about in a poisonous web of lies until the realistic and supernatural lines of action converge and he murders his second wife.
>
> Chris Dyer's set converts the theatre into a barn full of the rugged implements that define the character of Barry Kyle's production. If the cast are not otherwise engaged, they are churning, hauling sacks, tending bees, in a rhythm they can never afford to break under a threatening effigy that comes to sinister life during the Morris dances.
>
> Under the patronizing scrutiny of Frank's titled master, the dark side of rural England is brought fully into view.
>
> The Devil may appear as he does in the amazingly harnessed figure of Miles Anderson, who first stirs to life in an abandoned sack – but at the same time he is a projection by the community to explain everything that goes wrong with their lives.

Although he found Miriam Karlin's Mother Sawyer to be 'an entirely unmalignant figure who hatches out her little plots like practical jokes', Frank – who is pictured wearing a white robe with the word HOMICIDAL across the front – was the chief focus. 'The heart of the production lies in the performances of the bigamous trio. Gerard Murphy, Harriet Walter, and Juliet Stevenson present an extraordinary sense of passionate love unembittered by every-thing that happens including death. Even the two girls become devoted to each other. Mr. Murphy's writhing evasions between them – his use of elaborate imagery in contrast to their plain speech, and his pointing of the ominous ironies (worthy of Middleton) –

[27] Unsigned, *The Times* (of London), 22 May 1962, p. 15

Miles Anderson as Dog, Miriam Karlin as Elizabeth Sawyer, in
the Royal Shakespeare Company production of 1981 (photo:
Joe Cocks Studio, Stratford-upon-Avon)

L. to r.: behind table, George Raistrick as Carter, Robert
Eddison as Old Thorney, Simon Templeman as Warbeck; on
bench, Julia Hills as Anne Ratcliffe; on floor, John Burgess as
Old Banks, Anthony O'Donnell as Cuddy Banks; scene from
the Royal Shakespeare Company production of 1981 (photo:
Joe Cocks Studio, Stratford-upon-Avon)

take you emotionally every inch of the way up to the act of
murder.'[28]

For R. V. Holdsworth, Dog was the focus. 'There is no sellout to
farce or parody,' he comments in *TLS*. 'Miles Anderson as the Dog
is terrifying, slowly whipping his way from inside a harmless-look-
ing sack on a wheelbarrow for his first appearance (when, like
Mephistopheles to Faustus, he is accidentally summoned by Mother
Sawyer's cursing), looking on with ferocious intensity as Frank's
mind gradually receives the appalling knowledge that he is about to
murder his second wife, and suddenly stretching a long black arm
from beneath Frank's bed to put the blood-stained dagger in his
pocket.' From his perspective, 'Miriam Karlin's witch conveys a
poignant sense of defiant vulnerability and Gerard Murphy as
Frank has exactly the right blend of tenderness, cowardice, and
bewilderment'.[29] For James Fenton in the *Sunday Times*, the mes-
sage was largely political:

[28] *The Times* (of London), 17 September 1981, p. 9
[29] Holdsworth, p. 1099

The world evoked in this production, beautifully designed by Chris
Dyer, is one in which puritans and cavaliers mingle uneasily, where
'ridiculous old customs' still abound, where the hobby-horse has not
yet been forgotten. But we are asked to see this, I think, as a prelude to
a new England, where witchcraft will be stamped out, the Morris
Dance will be banned, and the theatre itself closed down. At the end of
the first half, the light falls on a primitive whirligig in the shape of a
puritan. The wooden figure waves its arms around its head, mechanical
and threatening. This is the best of Mr. Kyle's work that I have seen.

Such political significance is reinforced by songs added to the production. One, sung by the community of Edmonton as Mother
Sawyer first gathers sticks (II.i), is John Bunyan's translation of the
twenty-third Psalm: 'The God of love my shepherd is – / And he that
doth me feed, / Still He is mine and I am His, / What can I want
or need? / He leads me to the tender grass, / Where I both feed and
rest; / Then to the streams that gently pass: / In both I have the
best';[30] the attack on Mother Sawyer is, for Edmonton, justified.
But 'In Kyle's production,' Kathleen E. McLuskie notes, 'religious
superstition, seen as the source of injustice, was more emphasised
and the cast assembled to sing, ironically' yet another verse of a
hymn:

> The rich man in his castle
> The poor man at his gate
> He made them high and lowly
> And ordered their estate.[31]

Thus the community of works that dominates the stage at the play's
opening is forever locked into a regimented system that provides no
occupational alternatives.

Kyle's production as reconceived by the Acting Company of New
York City – a group founded in 1972 by John Houseman and
Margot Harley – was performed at the Shakespeare Theatre of the
Folger Shakespeare Library in Washington, D.C., from 29
September until 22 November 1987, before moving to New York.
Joel Fontaine redesigned the production along with Judith Dolan
(costumes), Nancy Schertler (lighting) and Roberta Gasbarre (chor-
eography); Scott Reiss directed the music. In this version Derek D.
Smith played Frank and Mary Lou Rosato was Mother Sawyer;
what was most notable, however, was its racial overtones. Two
African-Americans, Kim Staunton and Wendell Pierce, played
Winifred and 'A Black Dog' respectively.

---

[30] From the director's prompt-book, no p.
[31] Kathleen E. McLuskie, *Dekker and Heywood: Professional Dramatists* (London,
1994), pp. 148–9

Three other recent productions are recorded. In June 1984 the 1984 Graduates of the Old Vic Theatre School in Bristol supplied a black Dog with a Scottish accent, but the production itself fell short: 'The minute the Devil incarnate walks on stage any production is on thin ice and while here the demon stayed high and dry, the rest fell through.'[32] A 'workshop exploration' of the play was staged by the Equity Showcase Theatre in Toronto in 1991; when a full production was mounted during the first two weeks of December 1993, all of the cast but Greg Kramer, playing Dog, were women.[33]

Note on the Text

The Stationers' Register records that Edward Blackmore 'Entred for his Copie (under ye hand of M[r] Thomason Warden) a booke called The Witch of Edmonton a TragiComedy by Will: Rowley &c' on 21 May 1658, some 37 years after the source pamphlet of Henry Goodcole and the first recorded performances. The only extant edition of the play is a quarto of that year, which seems to have derived from a revival of the play in the 1630s since it includes the names of actors then belonging to Queen Henrietta Maria's Men – Theophilus Bird and Ezekiel Fenn as well as (presumably) Hamluc, Poldavis and W. Mago. Bentley (I, 251–2; II, 378; III, 271–2) conjectures a MS prompt copy of the revived production; Bowers (III, 483–6) argues for an autograph copy of 'a rather literal scribal copy preliminary to the prompt book'. But the quarto, with its irregular and often omitted stage directions, would seem at least one step removed from prompt-copy. That it is closely related to a theatrical script, however, is clear enough from the punctuation alone: unlike pointing even for its own time, the play reads phrasally and dramatically. The rather heavy pointing in places, in fact, would direct actors to slow down certain scenes, often those involving the actions with the highest dramatic pitch.

The quarto is often badly set and remains uncorrected in all the copies examined, arguing only one typesetting with no proof corrections: four pages are clearly misnumbered in Act V; act and scene divisions are inconsistent; prose and poetry are mixed (so that Mother Sawyer, for example, speaks in both); there are varying speech prefixes ('Young Banks' also appears as 'Clown'; 'Young Thorney' also appears as 'Frank'); and a number of words and even lines have become loose, with the Huntington Library copy, having the most worn type and the loosest lines, representing a late stage of the print-run.

---

[32] 'The Witch of Edmonton (New Vic)', *Bacus*, no date or page supplied. In the University of Bristol Theatre Collection

[33] From a copy of the programme for the 1993 production

For this edition, all eight known copies of the play were collated: British Library 644.c.17 (which was used as copy-text); British Library C.12. f.p.(5); Malone 238 at the Bodleian Library; D (Dyce) 25.C.70 at the Victoria and Albert; STR. 117/18 (Stoner Bequest) at Eton College; the copy at the Huntington Library; Harvard *14433.26.13* at the Houghton Library; and Yale 162 at the Elizabethan Club (which notes on the fly leaf, 'Extremely rare, & most interesting play'). Two other copies are actually ghosts: the copy catalogued at the Folger Shakespeare Library is a facsimile of the Huntington Library copy; the copy listed for the Furness Library at the University of Pennsylvania is a photostat of the Harvard copy. The quarto collates A^2;B–I^4: A1, title-page; A1v, blank; A2, actors names; A2v, distich and prologue; B1–I3v, text; I4, Epilogue; I4v, blank.

Textual editing is an act of mediation; all texts are essentially provisional. For the present text, all irregular speech prefixes, stage directions and typesetting errors (noted in the text) have been regularized, and abbreviations have been spelled out. In keeping with the principles of this series, words have been modernized (including Winnifride as Winifred) and italics and capitalizations removed. The pointing, however, is another matter: unlike other modern texts of this play which punctuate by twentieth-century practices, it seems clear that this is a theatrical text in which the punctuation often controls interpretation and delivery. Thus some speeches printed as questions in other editions are here restored to declarations; speeches are more often broken into phrases. For the most part, the signs for longer pauses in Stuart England (: and .) have both been treated as (.) to distinguish their time of pausing from (,) and (;). The intention has been to bring the text as close to its original performances as extant evidence will allow. References for proverbs are to Morris Palmer Tilley, *A Dictionary of Proverbs in England in the Sixteenth and Seventeenth Centuries* (Ann Arbor, 1950).

FURTHER READING

Barber, C. L., *Shakespeare's Festive Comedy* (Princeton, 1959)

Bentley, G. E., *The Jacobean and Caroline Stage* (Oxford, 1941–68)

Bowers, Fredson, ed., *The Dramatic Works of Thomas Dekker* (Cambridge, 1958), III, 481–568

Briggs, K. M., *Pale Hecate's Team* (London, 1962)

Comensoli, Viviana, *'Household Business': Domestic Plays of Early Modern England* (Toronto, 1996), 121–31

Conover, James H., *Thomas Dekker: An Analysis of Dramatic Structure* (The Hague, 1969)

Dolan, Frances E., *Dangerous Familiars: Representations of Domestic Crime in England 1550–1700* (Ithaca and London, 1994)

Edwards, Philip, G. E. Bentley, Kathleen McLuskie and Lois Potter, *The Revels History of Drama in English, Volume IV: 1613–1660* (London and New York, 1981)

George, David, 'Rushbearing: A Forgotten British Custom' in Johnston and Hüsken

Greenfield, Peter H., 'Parish Drama in Four Counties Bordering the Thames Watershed' in Johnston and Hüsken, pp. 106–18

Gregory, Anabel, 'Witchcraft, Politics, and "Good Neighbourhood" in Early Seventeenth-Century Rye', *Past and Present* 133 (November 1991), 31–66

Gurr, Andrew, *The Shakespearean Stage, 1574–1642*, 3rd edn (Cambridge, 1992)

Harris, Anthony, 'Instruments of Mischief' in *Night's Black Agents: Witchcraft and Magic in Seventeenth-Century English Drama* (Manchester, 1980), 90–108

Hoy, Cyrus, *Introductions, Notes, and Commentaries to Texts in the Dramatic Works of Thomas Dekker* (Cambridge, 1980)

Johnston, Alexandra F., '"What Revels are in Hand?": Dramatic Activities Sponsored by the Parishes of the Thames Valley' in Johnston and Hüsken, pp. 95–104

Johnston, Alexandra F. and Hüsken, Win, eds, *English Parish Drama* (Amsterdam, 1996)

King, T. J., 'Staging of Plays at the Phoenix in Drury Lane, 1617–42', *Theatre Notebook* XIX (1965), 146–66

Kishlansky, Mark, *A Monarchy Transformed: Britain 1603–1714* (London, 1996)

Larner, Christina, *Witchcraft and Religion: The Politics of Popular Belief* (Oxford, 1984)

Leech, Clifford, *John Ford and the Drama of his Time* (London, 1957)

Levin, Richard, 'Flower Maidens, Wise Women, Witches and the Gendering of Knowledge in English Renaissance Drama' in *Shakespeare's Universe: Renaissance Ideas and Conventions: Essays in honour of W. R. Elton*, eds John M. Mucciolo, Steven J. Doloff and Edward A. Rachut (London, 1996)

McLuskie, Kathleen E., *Dekker and Heywood: Professional Dramatists* (London, 1994)

Oliver, H. J., *The Problem of John Ford* (Melbourne, 1955)

Orlin, Lena Cowen, *Private Matters and Public Culture in Post-Reformation England* (Ithaca, 1994)

Price, G. R., *Thomas Dekker* (New York, 1969)

Purkiss, Diane, *The Witch in History: Early Modern and Twentieth-Century Representations* (London, 1996)

Rosen, Barbara, ed., *Witchcraft in England, 1558–1618*, 2nd edn (Amherst, 1991)

Sergeaunt, M. Joan, *John Ford* (Oxford, 1935)

Sugden, Edward Holdsworth, *A Topographical Dictionary to the Works of Shakespeare and His Fellow Dramatists* (London, 1925)

Thomas, Keith, *Religion and the Decline of Magic* (Harmondsworth, 1978, 1988)

Tilley, Morris Palmer, *A Dictionary of the Proverbs in England in the Sixteenth and Seventeenth Centuries. A Collection of the Proverbs Found in English Literature and the Dictionaries of the Period* (Ann Arbor, 1950)

Underdown, David, *A Freeborn People: Politics and the Nation in Seventeenth-Century England* (Oxford, 1996)

West, E. S., 'The Significance of *The Witch of Edmonton*', *Criterion* XVII (1937), 23–32

Wiggin, Pauline G., *An Inquiry into the Authorship of the Middleton-Rowley Plays* (Boston, 1897)

The Witch of Edmonton:

A known true STORY.

Composed into

A TRAGI-COMEDY

By divers well-esteemed Poets;

William Rowley, Thomas Dekker, John Ford, &c.

Acted by the Princes Servants, often at the Cock-Pit in *Drury-Lane*, once at Court, with singular Applause.

Never printed till now.

London, *Printed by* J. Cottrel, *for* Edward Blackmore, *at the Angel in* Paul's Church-yard. 1658.

First Edition.

Actors' Names

Sir Arthur Clarington
Old Thorney, a Gentleman
Old Carter, a rich Yeoman
Old Banks, a Countryman
W. Mago, } two Countrymen   5
W. Hamluc, }
Three other Countrymen
Warbeck, } suitors to [Old] Carter's daughters
Somerton, }
Frank, [Old] Thorney's son   10
Young Cuddy Banks, the Clown
Four Morris Dancers
Old Ratcliffe
Sawgut, an old Fiddler
Poldavis, a Barber's boy   15
Justice
Constable
Officers
Servingmen
Dog, a Familiar   20
A Spirit
Mother Sawyer, the Witch
Anne, [Old] Ratcliffe's Wife
Susan, } [Old] Carter's daughters
Katherine, }   25
Winifred, Sir Arthur's Maid
[Jane, a Maid]

---

4 *Old Banks* Sugden notes a Banks also appears as the Miller of Waltham in *The Merry Devil of Edmonton*; it 'seems to indicate that he was a study from life'

5 *W. Mago* Bentley identifies him as an actor in the King's Company in 1624 and 1631. He is named only twice, and both times elsewhere – as a 'Carthaginian Officer' and an attendant on the Prussian king in the King's Men's production of Massinger's *Believe as You List* (1631). Bowers argues that Mago and Hamluc (below) were members of Henrietta Maria's Men in the revival in the 1630s

6 *W. Hamluc* Bentley argues this is an error, listing an actor who is given two short speeches in IV.i

11 *Cuddy* derived from Cudden or fool, ass

15 *Poldavis* Probably an actor's name; he is referred to at III.i.59, but has no clear role and is not mentioned in the stage direction

The whole Argument is this Distich
Forced Marriage, Murder; Murder, Blood requires.
Reproach, Revenge; Revenge, Hell's help desires.

Distich couplet; line 1 gives precedent to the overplot; line 2, to the underplot

Prologue

The Town of Edmonton hath lent the Stage
A Devil and a Witch, both in an age.
To make comparisons it were uncivil,
Between so even a pair, a Witch and Devil.
But as the year doth with his plenty bring   5
As well a latter as a former Spring;
So has this Witch enjoyed the first, and reason
Presumes she may partake the other season.
In Acts deserving name, the Proverb says,
Once good, and ever; Why not so in Plays?   10
Why not in this? since (Gentlemen) we flatter
No Expectations. Here is Mirth and Matter.

Master Bird

Prologue Clearly written for a revival of the play c. 1635 when Theophilus Bird and
Ezekiel Fenn (Winifred) were both in Queen Henrietta's Company. Bentley and
Hoy speculate the revival was around 1635 at the Cockpit in London

1 *Edmonton* Then a village in Middlesex about 7 miles north of London

2 *Devil* Thought to refer to an earlier play, *The Merry Devil of Edmonton*, but see
also I.i.19. *The Merry Devil* was frequently staged and printed from 1608 to 1631
and is also referred to in two works of Middleton and two of Jonson; it was staged
by 1604 and given a performance at court in 1613. In 1653 the printer Humphrey
Moseley mistakenly attributed this anonymous work to Shakespeare. Performances and publication continued until 1691. The plot may well have influenced the
Thorney overplot (see Introduction)

12 *Matter* serious material

13 *Master Bird* Presumably the actor who spoke these lines, probably the son of
William Bird. He first played female roles, graduating to male roles by the 1630s;
with Andrew Penncuicke he signed the dedication to Dekker and Ford's *The Sun's
Darling*

THE WITCH OF EDMONTON

Act I, Scene i

Enter [YOUNG] FRANK THORNEY, WINIFRED *with child*

FRANK
    Come, wench; why here's a business soon dispatched.
    Thy heart I know is now at ease. Thou needst not
    Fear what the tattling gossips in their cups
    Can speak against thy fame. Thy child shall know
    Who to call Dad now.
WINIFRED   You have discharged   5
    The true part of an honest man; I cannot
    Request a fuller satisfaction
    Than you have freely granted. Yet methinks
    'Tis a hard case, being lawful man and wife,
    We should not live together.
FRANK   Had I failed   10
    In promise of my truth to thee, we must
    Have then been ever sundered; now the longest
    Of our forbearing either's company,
    Is only but to gain a little time
    For our continuing thrift, that so hereafter   15
    The heir that shall be born may not have cause
    To curse his hour of birth, which made him feel
    The misery of beggary and want;
    Two devils that are occasions to enforce

Scene i This scene – because of its style and situation – is generally attributed to Ford,
    but from the start of his career, Dekker was known for his structural craftsman-
    ship in beginning plays forcefully and thematically. Here the exposition of events
    previous to the play is skilfully released for dramatic effectiveness and irony
  0 s.d. 1 *with child* pregnant
  1 *wench* woman; here a neutral or even affectionate term
    dispatched taken care of
  3 *gossips* slang for newsmongers
    in their cups in drunkenness
 13 *forbearing* giving up
 15 *thrift* well-being
 19 *Two devils* Beggary and want link overplot and subplot here
    occasions causes

A shameful end. My plots aim but to keep   20
My father's love.
WINIFRED   And that will be as difficult
To be preserved, when he shall understand
How you are married, as it will be now,
Should you confess it to him.
FRANK   Fathers are
Won by degrees, not bluntly, as our masters   25
Or wronged friends are; and besides, I'll use
Such dutiful and ready means, that ere
He can have notice of what's past, th'inheritance
To which I am born heir shall be assured.
That done, why let him know it; if he likes it not,   30
Yet he shall have no power in him left
To cross the thriving of it.
WINIFRED   You who had
The conquest of my maiden-love, may easily
Conquer the fears of my distrust. And whither
Must I he hurried?
FRANK   Prithee do not use   35
A word so much unsuitable to the constant
Affections of thy husband. Thou shalt live
Near Waltham Abbey, with thy Uncle Selman.
I have acquainted him with all at large.
He'll use thee kindly. Thou shalt want no pleasures,   40
Nor any other fit supplies whatever
Thou canst in heart desire.
WINIFRED   All these are nothing
Without your company.
FRANK   Which thou shalt have
Once every month at least.
WINIFRED   Once every month!
Is this to have an husband?
FRANK   Perhaps oftener.   45
That's as occasion serves.
WINIFRED   Ay, ay; in case

---

32 *cross* prevent
33 *conquest of my maiden-love* ended my virginity (by conquering my maidenhead)
38 *Waltham Abbey* Then 12 miles north of London across the border from the vil-
     lage of Waltham, or Waltham Cross, Hertfordshire (see map on pp. xxiv–xxv)
39 *large* length
46 *Ay, ay* (I, I Q (quarto publication of the text))

No other beauty tempt your eye, whom you
Like better, I may chance to be remembered,
And see you now and then. Faith, I did hope
You'd not have used me so. 'Tis but my fortune.   50
And yet, if not for my sake, have some pity
Upon the child I go with, that's your own.
And, 'less you'll be a cruel-hearted father,
You cannot but remember that.
Heaven knows how –
FRANK   To quit which fear at once,   55
As by the ceremony late performed,
I plighted thee a faith, as free from challenge,
As any double thought; once more in hearing
Of heaven and thee, I vow, that never henceforth
Disgrace, reproof, lawless affections, threats,   60
Or what can be suggested 'gainst our marriage,
Shall cause me falsify that bridal oath
That binds me thine. And, Winifred, whenever
The wanton heat of youth by subtle baits
Of beauty, or what woman's art can practise,   65
Draw me from only loving thee; let heaven
Inflict upon my life some fearful ruin.
I hope thou dost believe me.
WINIFRED   Swear no more;
I am confirmed, and will resolve to do
What you think most behooveful for us.
FRANK   Thus then;   70
Make thyself ready. At the furthest house
Upon the green, without the town, your uncle
Expects you. For a little time farewell.
WINIFRED   Sweet,

---

50 *You'd* (Youl'd Q)

55 *how –* (how. Q)

57 *plighted* vowed

    plighted thee a faith In Rowley's *All's Lost for Lust* (c. 1607, published 1633),
    the nobleman Antonio pledges the country girl Marguerite to a secret marriage;
    as Frank will, he later denies the marriage by marrying a girl of a higher social
    class

58 *double* strong; also possibly duplicitous

67 *ruin* Ironic anticipation following Frank's betrayal of Winifred

69 *I am confirmed* Winifred's staunch loyalty to Frank will be complicated by later
    revelations

70 *most behooveful* advantageous

We shall meet again as soon as thou canst possibly?
FRANK
    We shall. One kiss. [*Kisses her*] Away.

                              [*Exit* WINIFRED]

              Enter SIR ARTHUR CLARINGTON

SIR ARTHUR   Frank Thorney.
FRANK   Here Sir.   75
SIR ARTHUR
    Alone? Then must I tell thee in plain terms,
    Thou hast wronged thy master's house basely and lewdly.
FRANK
    Your house, sir?
SIR ARTHUR   Yes, sir. If the nimble devil
    That wantoned in your blood rebelled against
    All rules of honest duty, you might, sir,   80
    Have found out some more fitting place than here
    To have built a stews in. All the country whispers
    How shamefully thou hast undone a maid,
    Approved for modest life, for civil carriage,
    Till thy prevailing perjuries enticed her   85
    To forfeit shame. Will you be honest yet?
    Make her amends and marry her?

74 s.d. *Sir* The basis of Clarington's title – and thus his precise social status – is
    never explained; it might derive from an hereditary baronetcy or an individual
    knighthood awarded for life. By 1621, however, the title no longer signified mili-
    tary or political service to the king and had become diluted by James I who sold
    the honour to produce royal income; he created more knights in his first four
    months in office than Elizabeth I had in her entire reign of 44 years. Here it has
    been used as a social marker to give Sir Arthur the highest social status in the
    play (cf. V.iii.157 ff.) and thus potentially the most exploitative

77 *Thou* A formal and more distant term used to address lower classes
    thy master's That a gentleman like Frank is in service to Sir Arthur as an eldest
    (or only) rather than a younger son indicates his father's low financial state. Boys
    and girls normally entered service between the ages of 12 and 15; length and
    terms of service varied with the master, as well as treatment, from strict author-
    itarianism to developing dependency. If girls did not marry when their term of
    service ended, they often stayed on with their employer. Frank's ability here to
    keep his distance from Sir Arthur (unlike Winifred) argues for his difference in
    gender, class and possibly maturity

82 *stews* brothel

84 *civil* courteous, proper

85 *prevailing perjuries* successful false arguments

FRANK   So, sir,
   I might bring both myself and her to beggary;
   And that would be a shame worse than the other.
SIR ARTHUR
   You should have thought on this before, and then   90
   Your reason would have overswayed the passion
   Of your unruly lust. But that you may
   Be left without excuse, to salve the infamy
   Of my disgraced house, and 'cause you are
   A gentleman, and both of you my servants,   95
   I'll make the maid a portion.
FRANK   So you promised me
   Before, in case I married her. I know
   Sir Arthur Clarington deserves the credit
   Report hath lent him; and presume you are
   A debtor to your promise. But upon   100
   What certainty shall I resolve? Excuse me
   For being somewhat rude.
SIR ARTHUR   'Tis but reason.
   Well, Frank, what thinkest thou of two hundred pound
   And a continual friend?
FRANK   Though my poor fortunes
   Might happily prefer me to a choice   105
   Of a far greater portion; yet to right
   A wronged maid, and to preserve your favour,
   I am content to accept your proffer.
SIR ARTHUR   Art thou?
FRANK
   Sir, we shall every day have need to employ
   The use of what you please to give.
SIR ARTHUR   Thou shalt hav't.   110
FRANK
   Then I claim your promise. We are man and wife.
SIR ARTHUR
   Already?
FRANK   And more than so, I have promised her
   Free entertainment in her uncle's house,
   Near Waltham Abbey, where she may securely
   Sojourn, till time and my endeavours work   115

---

92 *But that* because
95 *gentleman* Children of gentry were often educated by serving in households of
   social superiors; Sir Arthur's generosity will soon reveal darker motives
96 *portion* dowry
100–1 *But … resolve?* How should I be certain?
113 *entertainment* hospitality

My father's love and liking.
SIR ARTHUR   Honest Frank.
FRANK
I hope, sir, you will think I cannot keep her
Without a daily charge.
SIR ARTHUR   As for the money,
'Tis all thine own; and though I cannot make thee
A present payment, yet thou shalt be sure   120
I will not fail thee.
FRANK   But our occasions –
SIR ARTHUR   Nay, nay,
Talk not of your occasions, trust my bounty.
It shall not sleep. Hast married her, i'faith, Frank?
'Tis well, 'tis passing well. [*Aside*] Then Winifred,
Once more thou art an honest woman. [*To* FRANK] Frank,   125
Thou hast a jewel. Love her, she'll deserve it.
And when to Waltham?
FRANK   She is making ready.
Her uncle stays for her.
SIR ARTHUR   Most provident speed.
Frank, I will be thy friend, and such a friend.
Thou'lt bring her thither?
FRANK   Sir, I cannot. Newly   130
My father sent me word I should come to him.
SIR ARTHUR
Marry, and do. I know thou hast a wit
To handle him.
FRANK   I have a suit t'ye.
SIR ARTHUR   What is't?
Anything, Frank, command it.
FRANK   That you'll please
By letters to assure my father that   135
I am not married.
SIR ARTHUR   How?
FRANK   Some one or other
Hath certainly informed him that I purposed
To marry Winifred, on which he threatened
To disinherit me; to prevent it,

---

120 *present payment* Cf. V.iii.158; presumably Sir Arthur is not telling Frank the
    truth, whereas he will the Justice
121 *occasions* – (occasions. Q) needs
128 *stays* waits
130 *Newly* just now
132 *Marry* A term of strong agreement
133 *suit* request (of a social superior)

Lowly I crave your letters, which he seeing 140
Will credit; and I hope, ere I return,
On such conditions as I'll frame, his lands
Shall be assured.
SIR ARTHUR   But what is there to quit
My knowledge of the marriage?
FRANK   Why you were not
A witness to it.
SIR ARTHUR   I conceive. And then, 145
His land confirmed, thou wilt acquaint him thoroughly
With all that's passed.
FRANK   I mean no less.
SIR ARTHUR   Provided,
I never was made privy to it.
FRANK   Alas, sir,
Am I a talker?
SIR ARTHUR   Draw thyself the letter,
I'll put my hand to it. I commend thy policy. 150
Thou'rt witty, witty Frank; nay, nay, 'tis fit,
Dispatch it.
FRANK
I shall write effectually.   *Exit*
SIR ARTHUR
Go thy way, cuckoo; have I caught the young man?
One trouble then is freed. He that will feast 155
At others' cost, must be a bold-faced guest.

Enter WINIFRED *in a riding suit*

I have heard the news, all now is safe,
The worst is past. Thy lip, wench. [*Kisses her*] I must bid

140 *Lowly* humbly
143 *assured* secured (for myself)
143–4 *But ... marriage?* What grounds do I have not to know about the marriage?
145 *conceive* understand
148 *made privy to* given knowledge of
149–50 *Draw ... it.* Write the letter; I'll sign it
150 *policy* strategy
151 *witty* crafty
154 *cuckoo* (Cuckow Q, as homonym to cuckold) cuckold; also slang for fool; Sir
    Arthur's character is first revealed here (cf. 194–6 below)
    caught trapped
157–8 *I ... past.* (*Winifred* Q) This speech prefix must be in error; the conspiratorial
    tone is in keeping with Sir Arthur's attitude but is never shown by Winifred. Her
    situation resembles that of Jacinta in Rowley's *All's Lost by Lust*; Dekker treats
    adultery in *The Honest Whore Part II*

Farewell, for fashion's sake; but I will visit thee
Suddenly, girl. This was cleanly carried.   160
Ha, was't not Win?

WINIFRED   Then were my happiness,
That I in heart repent I did not bring him
The dower of virginity. Sir, forgive me;
I have been much to blame. Had not my lewdness
Given way to your immoderate waste of virtue,   165
You had not with such eagerness pursued
The error of your goodness.

SIR ARTHUR   Dear, dear Win.
I hug this art of thine, it shows how cleanly
Thou canst beguile, in case occasion serve
To practise. It becomes thee, now we share   170
Free scope enough, without control or fear,
To interchange our pleasures; we will surfeit
In our embraces, wench. Come, tell me, when
Wilt thou appoint a meeting?

WINIFRED   What to do?

SIR ARTHUR

Good, good, to con the lesson of our loves,   175
Our secret game.

160 *Suddenly* very soon
     cleanly carried well done
161–4 *Then ... blame* Winifred's change of heart suggests moral transformation and
     underscores Sir Arthur's continuing complicity
164 *lewdness* (laundress Q)
164–7 *Had not ... goodness* Had not my lust surrendered to your advances, you had
     not so eagerly pursued this bad behaviour. While consummation before or out-
     side marriage was not sanctioned, it was also not uncommon
169 *Thou canst beguile* Sir Arthur thinks Winifred has decided to marry Frank to
     conceal the truth of her pregnancy and continue their affair; the rest of this scene
     encodes lines about their liaison
     beguile, (beguile Q)
170 *practise* scheme, plot
     becomes suits
175 *con* learn, memorise
175–8 *con ... monstrous* Sir Arthur sees this marriage as a way to pursue his sexual
     alliance with Winifred – something Frank does not know – but following her
     marriage she declines any further relationship with Sir Arthur. The tragedy of the
     couple stems from this interchange
176 *Our secret* Sir Arthur sees his alliance as sport. In 1633 – after the play was writ-
     ten but before it was printed – Archbishop Laud introduced the punishment of
     such adulterous nobility by requiring them to stand in a white sheet before the
     congregation of their parish church as a sign of their sexual misconduct

WINIFRED   O blush to speak it further!
  As y'are a noble gentleman, forget
  A sin so monstrous. 'Tis not gently done,
  To open a cured wound. I know you speak
  For trial; troth, you need not.
SIR ARTHUR   I for trial?   180
  Not I, by this good sunshine!
WINIFRED   Can you name
  That syllable of good, and yet not tremble,
  To think to what a foul and black intent,
  You use it for an oath? Let me resolve you,
  If you appear in any visitation   185
  That brings not with it pity for the wrongs
  Done to abused Thorney, my kind husband;
  If you infect mine ear with any breath
  That is not thoroughly perfumed with sighs
  For former deeds of lust, may I be cursed   190
  Even in my prayers, when I vouchsafe
  To see or hear you. I will change my life,
  From a loose whore to a repentant wife.
SIR ARTHUR
  Wilt thou turn monster now? Are not ashamed
  After so many months to be honest at last?   195
  Away, away, fie on't!
WINIFRED   My resolution
  Is built upon a rock. This very day
  Young Thorney vowed with oaths not to be doubted,
  That never any change of love should cancel
  The bonds, in which we are to either bound,   200
  Of lasting truth. And shall I then for my part
  Unfile the sacred oath set on record
  In heaven's book? Sir Arthur, do not study
  To add to your lascivious lust the sin
  Of sacrilege. For if you but endeavour   205
  By any unchaste word to tempt my constancy,
  You strive as much as in you lies to ruin
  A temple hallowed to the purity
  Of holy marriage. I have said enough.
  You may believe me.

184 *resolve you* end your doubts
190 *lust,* (lust: Q)
191 *vouchsafe* allow myself
202 *Unfile* retract
203 *study* attempt

SIR ARTHUR   Get you to your nunnery,   210
  There freeze in your cold cloister. This is fine.
WINIFRED
  Good angels guide me. Sir you'll give me leave
  To weep and pray for your conversion?
SIR ARTHUR   Yes,
  Away to Waltham! Pox on your honesty.
  Had you no other trick to fool me? Well,   215
  You may want money yet.
WINIFRED   None that I'll send for
  To you, for hire of a damnation.
  When I am gone, think on my just complaint.
  I was your devil, O be you my saint!   *Exit* WIN[IFRED]
SIR ARTHUR
  Go, go thy ways, as changeable a baggage   220
  As ever cozened knight. I'm glad I'm rid of her.
  Honest? Marry, hang her! Thorney is my debtor,
  I thought to have paid him too. But fools have fortune.
                                   Exit S[IR] A[RTHUR]

Act I, Scene ii

Enter OLD THORNEY, *and* OLD CARTER

OLD THORNEY
  You offer, Master Carter, like a gentleman;
  I cannot find fault with it, 'tis so fair.

210 *Get . . . nunnery* Probably an allusion to *Hamlet* III.i.120
211 *cold* (old Q)
223 *fine* cunning
214 *Pox* syphilis; plague (an idiomatic term of annoyance)
217 *for hire of a* to be rewarded with
220 *baggage* immoral woman
221 *cozened* cheated
222 *Marry,* (Marry Q) A term of surprise; originally an oath, 'By the Virgin Mary'
223 *fools have fortune* Proverbial; F536 (Tilley)

  1 *offer* Old Thorney's arrangement of his son's marriage, like Old Carter's of his
     daughter's, is not unusual among aristocrats and gentry nor is it unkind; Old
     Thorney will not only regain solvency but assure Frank of an inheritance
     like a gentleman The play continues to make social class an issue, but here the
     scene reverses I.i: whereas Sir Arthur used his superior status to subjugate Frank
     and Winifred, Old Thorney pleads with his yeoman inferior Old Carter by flat-
     tering him with this form of address
     gentleman; (gentleman, Q)

OLD CARTER
  No gentleman I, Master Thorney; spare the Mastership,
  call me by my name, John Carter; Master is a title my
  father, nor his before him, were acquainted with. Honest   5
  Hertfordshire yeomen, such an one am I; my word and my
  deed shall be proved one at all times. I mean to give you no
  security for the marriage-money.

OLD THORNEY
  How? No security?
  Although it need not, so long as you live;   10
  Yet who is he has surety of his life one hour?
  Men, the proverb says, are mortal. Else, for my part,
  I distrust you not, were the sum double.

OLD CARTER
  Double, treble, more or less; I tell you, Master Thorney, I'll
  give no security. Bonds and bills are but tarriers to catch   15
  fools, and keep lazy knaves busy; my security shall be present payment. And we here, about Edmonton, hold present
  payment as sure as an alderman's bond in London, Master
  Thorney.

OLD THORNEY
  I cry you mercy, sir, I understand you not.   20

OLD CARTER
  I like young Frank well, so does my Susan too. The girl has
  a fancy to him, which makes me ready in my purse. There
  be other suitors within, that make much noise to little purpose. If Frank love Sue, Sue shall have none but Frank. 'Tis
  a mannerly girl, Master Thorney, though but an homely   25

  6 *Hertfordshire* Old Carter reliably lays claim to being a local landlord of some
    means
    yeomen farming class; Thomas Wilson in 1601 distinguishes yeoman class and
    below from aristocrats and gentry because they labour with their hands
  7 *give you* require
 12 *Men ... mortal* Proverbial; M502
 15–16 *Bonds ... busy* Dekker in particular was concerned with mercantile arrange-
    ments; but interest in the power of capital was by this time becoming common-
    place
 15 *tarriers* obstructions; hindrances
 16–17 *present* immediate
 18 *alderman* governing authority
 20 *I ... mercy* I beg forgiveness; Old Thorney's sense of status has harboured a mis-
    trust of yeomen generally, but here it would defeat his purpose
 22 *ready in my purse* willing to pay the dowry; Old Carter maintains his dignity at
    the proposal of improved social status by marriage; his continual use of proverbs
    betrays his lower social status throughout

man's daughter. There have worse faces looked out of
black bags, man.

OLD THORNEY

You speak your mind freely and honestly.
I marvel my son comes not. I am sure he will be
Here sometime today.   30

OLD CARTER

Today or tomorrow, when he comes he shall be welcome to
bread, beer, and beef, yeoman's fare; we have no kickshaws. Full dishes, whole bellyfulls. Should I diet three days
at one of the slender city-suppers, you might send me to
Barber-Surgeons' Hall the fourth day, to hang up for an   35
anatomy. Here come they that –

Enter WARBECK *with* SUSAN, SOMERTON *with*
KATHERINE

How now girls? Every day play-day with you? Valentine's
day too, all by couples? Thus will young folks do when we
are laid in our graves, Master Thorney. Here's all the care
they take. And how do you find the wenches, gentlemen?   40
Have they any mind to a loose gown and a strait shoe? Win
'em, and wear 'em. They shall choose for themselves by my
consent.

27 *bags* Perhaps masks worn by women out of doors to protect complexions and
   indoors at balls and banquets; see *Measure for Measure* II.iv.94
28–30 (set as prose Q)
32 *yeoman's fare* Old Carter is self-conscious about his class while insisting he is a
   good provider
32–3 *kickshaws* fancy food (from French *quelque chose*). This speech complicates
   Old Carter's character; having located a suitor for Katherine as far away as West
   Ham and being willing to dismiss the engagement of Susan to Warbeck for a
   better match with Frank, Old Carter is essentially selfish, a good provider in a
   double sense
35 *Barber-Surgeons* Trade guild of men who performed simple operations; their
   Hall was built in Monkswell Street near Cripplegate in the reign of Edward IV
   as a special place for the dissection of corpses, and, in some instances, for the
   preservation of skeletons
36 *anatomy* skeleton, or a skeleton with its skin still remaining
36 s.d. (set one line later Q) A visual clue subsequent events will challenge
37–8 *Valentine's day* 14 February, a traditional time for the mating of birds
41 *loose gown* Probably a sexual joke
41–2 *Win 'em, and wear 'em* Proverbial; cf. 'woo her, win her, wear her' (W408)
   with *wear* meaning consummation
42–3 *by my consent* Old Carter's confession of his social and economic ambitions;
   he has, however, already opposed Warbeck in his agreement with Old Thorney

WARBECK
  You speak like a kind father. Sue, thou hearest
  The liberty that's granted thee. What sayest thou?   45
  Wilt thou be mine?
SUSAN   Your what, sir? I dare swear,
  Never your wife.
WARBECK   Canst thou be so unkind?
  Considering how dearly I affect thee;
  Nay, dote on thy perfections.
SUSAN   You are studied
  Too scholar-like in words I understand not.   50
  I am too coarse for such a gallant's love
  As you are.
WARBECK   By the honour of gentility –
SUSAN
  God sir, no swearing. Yea and nay with us
  Prevails above all oaths you can invent.
WARBECK
  By this white hand of thine –
SUSAN   Take a false oath?   55
  Fie, fie, flatter the wise. Fools not regard it;
  And one of these am I.
WARBECK   Dost thou despise me?
OLD CARTER
  Let 'em talk on, Master Thorney. I know Sue's mind. The
  fly may buzz about the candle, he shall but singe his wings
  when all's done. Frank, Frank is he has her heart.   60
SOMERTON
  But shall I live in hope, Kate?
KATHERINE
  Better so, than be a desperate man.

47 *Never your wife* Old Carter's previous line suggests Susan is in on his plan with
  Old Thorney
48 *affect* love
49 *Nay, dote* A construction familiar in Ford's work and grounds on which this
  scene has been at least partially attributed to him
51 *gallant* as a social ne'er-do-well
52 *gentility* Warbeck claims the same social status as Frank Thorney
53 *no swearing* Susan's sharp wit with Warbeck counters her earlier self-description
  (lines 49–52) and its later absence with Frank signals her serious interest in him
  Yea and nay A particularly serious oath (derived from Matthew 5:37)
59 *fly ... wings* Proverbial; F394

SOMERTON
  Perhaps thou thinkest it is thy portion
  I level at. Wert thou as poor in fortunes
  As thou art rich in goodness, I would rather   65
  Be suitor for the dower of thy virtues
  Than twice thy father's whole estate; and prithee
  Be thou resolved so.
KATHERINE   Master Somerton,
  It is an easy labour to deceive
  A maid that will believe men's subtle promises.   70
  Yet I conceive of you as worthily
  As I presume you do deserve.
SOMERTON   Which is
  As worthily in loving thee sincerely,
  As thou art worthy to be so beloved.
KATHERINE
  I shall find time to try you.
SOMERTON   Do, Kate, do.   75
  And when I fail, may all my joys forsake me.
OLD CARTER
  Warbeck and Sue are at it still. I laugh to myself, Master
  Thorney, to see how earnestly he beats the bush, while the
  bird is flown into another's bosom. A very unthrift, Master
  Thorney, one of the country roaring-lads. We have such as   80
  well as the city, and as arrant rake-hells as they are, though
  not so nimble at their prizes of wit. Sue knows the rascal to
  an hair's breadth, and will fit him accordingly.
OLD THORNEY
  What is the other gentleman?

63–8 *Perhaps … so* Somerton senses the importance of status in courting Old
    Carter's other daughter; he may be responding directly to the previous conver-
    sation between Warbeck and Susan
64 *level* aim
67 *prithee* Shortened version of 'I pray thee'
75 *try* test
78–9 *he … bosom* Proverbial; B740
79 *unthrift* (and therefore undeserving); Old Carter will not lose the prospect of a
    better marriage for Susan
80 *country roaring-lads* Such riotous young men were usually associated with
    London; perhaps his accusation is meant to appear false
81 *arrant rake-hells* dissolute rascals
82 *prizes* contests
    Sue Old Carter gives to his daughter interest in arranging a good match
83 *fit* reward

OLD CARTER
  One Somerton, the honester man of the two, by five pound   85
  in every stone-weight. A civil fellow. He has a fine con-
  venient estate of land in West Ham by Essex. Master
  Ranges, that dwells by Enfield, sent him hither. He likes
  Kate well. I may tell you, I think she likes him as well. If
  they agree, I'll not hinder the match for my part. But that   90
  Warbeck is such another –. I use him kindly for Master
  Somerton's sake, for he came hither first as a companion of
  his. Honest men, Master Thorney, may fall into knaves'
  company, now and then.
WARBECK
  Three hundred a year jointure, Sue.   95
SUSAN
  Where lies it, by sea or by land? I think by sea.
WARBECK
  Do I look a captain?
SUSAN   Not a whit, sir.
  Should all that use the seas be reckoned captains,
  There's not a ship should have a scullion in her
  To keep her clean.
WARBECK   Do you scorn me, Mistress Susan?   100
  Am I subject to be jeered at?
SUSAN   Neither
  Am I property for you to use
  As stale to your fond wanton loose discourse.
  Pray sir be civil.
WARBECK   Wilt be angry, wasp?

---

86 *stone-weight* 14 pounds; Old Carter is thus sceptical of Warbeck
87 *West Ham* Then a village 4½ miles north of London; this distinction is what
    seems to make him attractive to Old Carter, 'the honester man of the two' (85)
    by near, bordering on
88 *Enfield* Then about 11 miles from London in Middlesex (see map on pp.
    xxiv–xxv)
92 *sake,* (sake: Q)
93–4 *Honest … company* Proverbial; BM528
95 *Three … jointure* Joint ownership of his income of £300 a year with a provision
    for her if she is widowed
96 *by sea* That is, the fortune is less certain
103 *stale* decoy; pretext
    fond foolish
104 *Wilt … wasp?* 'As angry as a wasp' (Proverbial; W76)

OLD CARTER
God-a-mercy, Sue. She'll firk him on my life, if he fumble   105
with her.

Enter FRANK

Master Francis Thorney, you are welcome indeed. Your
father expected your coming. How does the right worship-
ful knight, Sir Arthur Clarington, your master?
FRANK
In health this morning. Sir, my duty.
OLD THORNEY   Now   110
You come as I could wish.
WARBECK   Frank Thorney, ha!
SUSAN
You must excuse me.
FRANK   Virtuous Mistress Susan.
Kind Mistress Katherine. Gentlemen, to both *Salutes them*
Good time o'th' day.
SOMERTON   The like to you.
WARBECK   'Tis he.
A word, friend [*To* SOMERTON] On my life, this is the man 115
Stands fair in crossing Susan's love to me.
SOMERTON
[*To* WARBECK] I think no less. Be wise, and take no notice
   on't.
He that can win her, best deserves her.
WARBECK   [*To* SOMERTON] Marry
A serving-man? Mew.
SOMERTON   [*To* WARBECK] Prithee friend no more.
OLD CARTER
Gentlemen all, there's within a slight dinner ready, if you 120
please to taste of it. Master Thorney, Master Francis,
Master Somerton. Why, girls? What, huswives, will you
spend all your forenoon in tittle-tattles? Away. It's well,
i'faith. Will you go in, gentlemen?

105 *God-a-mercy* God have mercy (a phrase of approval)
     firk beat
     fumble grope
110 *my duty* Signal that he bows in courtesy
113 s.d. *Salutes* greets with a kiss
116 *crossing* getting in the way of
119 *Mew* a word of social contempt
122 *huswives* loose women (a term of contempt)
123 *tittle-tattles* gossip

OLD THORNEY
    We'll follow presently. My son and I   125
    Have a few words of business.
OLD CARTER   At your pleasure.

                              Ex[eunt] the rest

OLD THORNEY
    I think you guess the reason, Frank, for which
    I sent for you.
FRANK   Yes, sir.
OLD THORNEY   I need not tell you
    With what a labyrinth of dangers daily
    The best part of my whole estate's encumbered.   130
    Nor have I any clew to wind it out,
    But what occasion proffers me. Wherein
    If you should falter, I shall have the shame,
    And you the loss. On these two points rely
    Our happiness or ruin. If you marry   135
    With wealthy Carter's daughter, there's a portion
    Will free my land. All which I will instate
    Upon the marriage to you. Otherwise,
    I must be of necessity enforced
    To make a present sale of all. And yet,   140
    For ought I know, live in as poor distress,
    Or worse, than now I do. You hear the sum.
    I told you thus before. Have you consider'd on't?
FRANK
    I have, sir. And however I could wish
    To enjoy the benefit of single freedom,   145
    For that I find no disposition in me
    To undergo the burden of that care
    That marriage brings with it; yet to secure
    And settle the continuance of your credit,
    I humbly yield to be directed by you   150

---

131 *clew* a ball of thread
    wind it out discover (referring to the thread Theseus unwound when entering the
    Minotaur's labyrinth so that he could later find his way back out by following
    it)
134 *you the loss* Old Thorney's reasoning includes securing his son's future, but the
    appeal is also aimed at Frank's self-interest
137 *instate* bestow
148–50 *secure . . . you* Frank assigns responsibility for his bigamous act to his father's
    wishes, as Old Carter has assigned any blame to Susan

In all commands.
OLD THORNEY   You have already used
  Such thriving protestations to the maid,
  That she is wholly yours. And speak the truth,
  You love her, do you not?
FRANK   'Twere pity, sir,
  I should deceive her.
OLD THORNEY   Better y'had been unborn.   155
  But is your love so steady that you mean,
  Nay, more, desire to make her your wife?
FRANK   Else, sir,
  It were a wrong not to be righted.
OLD THORNEY   True,
  It were. And you will marry her?
FRANK   Heaven prosper it.
  I do intend it.
OLD THORNEY   O thou art a villain!   160
  A devil like a man! Wherein have I
  Offended all the powers so much, to be
  Father to such a graceless godless son?
FRANK
  To me, sir, this? O my cleft heart!
OLD THORNEY   To thee,
  Son of my curse. Speak with truth, and blush, thou mon-
    ster,   165
  Hast thou not married Winifred, a maid
  Was fellow-servant with thee?
FRANK   [*Aside*] Some swift spirit
  Has blown this news abroad. I must outface it.
OLD THORNEY
  D'you study for excuse? Why all the country
  Is full on't.
FRANK   With your licence, 'tis not charitable,   170
  I am sure it is not fatherly, so much
  To be o'erswayed with credulous conceit
  Of mere impossibilities. But fathers
  Are privileged to think and talk at pleasure.

168 *outface* boldly deny
169 *study* search
170 *full on't* aware of it
    licence permission
172 *conceit* imagination

OLD THORNEY
    Why canst thou yet deny thou hast no wife?   175
FRANK
    What do you take me for? An atheist?
    One that nor hopes the blessedness of life
    Hereafter, neither fears the vengeance due
    To such as make the marriage-bed an inn,
    Which travellers day and night,   180
    After a toilsome lodging leave at pleasure?
    Am I become so insensible of losing
    The glory of creation's work? My soul!
    O, I have lived too long!
OLD THORNEY   Thou hast, dissembler;
    Darest thou persevere yet? and pull down wrath   185
    As hot as flames of hell, to strike thee quick
    Into the grave of horror? I believe thee not.
    Get from my sight.
FRANK   Sir, though mine innocence
    Needs not a stronger witness than the clearness
    Of an unperished conscience; yet for that   190
    I was informed, how mainly you had been
    Possessed of this untruth. To quit all scruple
    Please you peruse this letter. 'Tis to you.
OLD THORNEY
    From whom?
FRANK   Sir Arthur Clarington my master.
OLD THORNEY
    Well, sir. [*Reads letter*]
FRANK   [*Aside*] On every side I am distracted,   195
    Am waded deeper into mischief,
    Than virtue can avoid. But on I must.
    Fate leads me. I will follow. [*To his father*] There you read

---

176 *atheist* one without any scruples
179 *marriage-bed an inn* That is, marriage as a night of sexual bliss only
180 *Which ... night* The short line may indicate some corruption in the text, but it
    makes sense and emendation seems unwise
186 *quick* living
190 *unperished* clear
191 *mainly* strongly
192 *quit* get rid of
197 *Than ... avoid* Frank continues to avoid full self-knowledge by seeing himself as
    virtuous and only wrong in his choice, 'mischief' (196); this line introduces a par-
    allel to Mother Sawyer who will see herself as forced to make a pact with Dog
    because of other people's attitudes (cf. II.i.1–2)

What may confirm you.
OLD THORNEY   Yes, and wonder at it.
    Forgive me, Frank. Credulity abused me.   200
    My tears express my joy. And I am sorry
    I injured innocence.
FRANK   Alas! I knew
    Your rate and grief proceeded from your love
    To me. So I conceived it.
OLD THORNEY   My good son.
    I'll bear with many faults in thee hereafter.   205
    Bear thou with mine.
FRANK   The peace is soon concluded.

Enter OLD CARTER [*and* SUSAN]

OLD CARTER
    Why, Master Thorney, d'ye mean to talk out your dinner?
    The company attends your coming. What must it be,
    Master Frank, or son Frank? I am plain Dunstable.
OLD THORNEY
    Son, brother, if your daughter like to have it so.   210
FRANK
    I dare be confident she's not altered
    From what I left her at our parting last.
    Are you, fair maid?
SUSAN   You took too sure possession
    Of an engaged heart.
FRANK   Which now I challenge.
OLD CARTER
    Marry and much good may it do thee, son. Take her to   215
    thee. Get me a brace of boys at a burden, Frank. The nurs-
    ing shall not stand thee in a pennyworth of milk. Reach her
    home and spare not. When's the day?

199 *confirm* convince
199–202 *Yes … innocence* (prose Q)
204 *conceived* understood
209 *plain Dunstable* Proverbial for direct, plainspoken, after the Dunstable–London
    road known for its straight and even route (D646)
210 *Son, brother* son-in-law, brother-in-law
214 *engaged heart* heart already won
    challenge claim
216 *brace* pair   *boys* That is, grandsons
    at a burden at the same time
216–17 *nursing … milk* the cost of nursing will not be yours
217 *Reach* take
218 *spare not* waste no time

OLD THORNEY

Tomorrow, if you please. To use ceremony
Of charge and custom, were to little purpose.   220
Their loves are married fast enough already.

OLD CARTER

A good motion. We'll e'en have an household dinner; and
let the fiddlers go scrape. Let the bride and bridegroom
dance at night together. No matter for the guests.
Tomorrow, Sue, tomorrow. Shall's to dinner now?   225

OLD THORNEY

We are on all sides pleased, I hope.

SUSAN

Pray heaven I may deserve the blessing sent me.
Now my heart is settled.

FRANK   So is mine.

OLD CARTER

Your marriage-money shall be received before your
wedding-shoes can be pulled on. Blessing on you both.   230

FRANK

[*Aside*] No man can hide his shame from heaven that
  views him.
In vain he flees, whose destiny pursues him.

Exeunt All

220 *Of ... purpose* By village custom, there should be a waiting period and public
   announcements of their intentions (banns). This unseemly haste of both parents
   and children will contribute to the tragedy (a variant on *Romeo and Juliet*); cf.
   Mother Sawyer's swift reaction to Old Banks (II.i)

222 *motion* proposal

223 *let ... scrape* dismiss the musicians. The Fiddler, later assigned to a morris dance,
   will (by parallel) be dismissed when he is replaced by Dog

224 *dance at night* May allude to the common tune 'The Shaking of the Sheets' with
   its sexual overtones

225 *Shall's* shall we (contraction of 'shall us')

232 *destiny* Frank defines destiny as guilt, not fate, concerning his agreement to
   marry Susan

Act II, Scene i

Enter ELIZABETH SAWYER, *gathering sticks*

SAWYER
And why on me? Why should the envious world
Throw all their scandalous malice upon me?
'Cause I am poor, deformed and ignorant,
And like a bow buckled and bent together,
By some more strong in mischiefs than myself?   5
Must I for that be made a common sink,
For all the filth and rubbish of men's tongues
To fall and run into? Some call me witch;
And being ignorant of myself, they go
About to teach me how to be one: urging   10
That my bad tongue (by their bad usage made so)
Forespeaks their cattle, doth bewitch their corn,

1-2 *why ... me?* Mother Sawyer sees her virtue displaced by the accusations of
others and herself as a hopeless victim despite her good intentions. Her social
oppression is the kind of role that Dekker specialized in throughout his career,
beginning with his first surviving play, *Old Fortunatus*, in 1599. Mother Sawyer
has most of the soliloquies in this play, emphasizing her social isolation. More
strangely, given her class, her lines are largely in poetry rather than prose, and
all are given as poetry here

3-4 *'Cause ... together* Goodcole writes that 'Her body was crooked and
deformed, even bending together' (sig. A4v); 'she was a very ignorant woman'
(sig. C1). Mother Sawyer's sympathetic characterization may therefore owe even
more to Reginald Scot's description of witches generally in *The Discouerie of
Witchcraft* as 'women who are commonly old, lame, blear-eied, pale, fowle, and
full of wrinkles; poore, sullen, superstitious ... They are leane and deformed,
shewing melancholie in their faces ... They are doting, scolds, mad, divelish'
(1.3). She is thus unlike the title character of Middleton's *The Witch* (1615–16)
whom the Mermaid editor finds a 'fantastic', 'tongue-in-cheek caricature' (p. xx)

6 *sink* pit for sewage

11 *That ... so* The witch was known for the power of her tongue and her speeches
were often considered curses; cf. Shakespeare's Caliban on Prospero (I.ii.365–6)
bad usage Thomas notes (p. 674) that powerless women might assume the position of witch to gain some authority and even respect in the community; cf.
George Gifford, *A Dialogue Concerning Witches and Witchcraftes* (1593), sig.
B1

12 *Forespeaks* bewitches

12–13 *Forespeaks ... nurse* According to Goodcole, Mother Sawyer confessed that
'I have bene by the helpe of the Divell, the meanes of many Christians and beasts
death; the cause that moved mee to do it, was malice and envy, for if any body
had angred me in any manner, I would be so revenged of them and of their

Themselves, their servants and their babes at nurse.
This they enforce upon me. And in part
Make me to credit it. And here comes one   15
Of my chief adversaries.

Enter OLD BANKS

OLD BANKS
Out, out upon thee, witch.
SAWYER   Dost call me witch?
OLD BANKS
I do, witch, I do. And worse I would, I knew I a name more
hateful. What makest thou upon my ground?
SAWYER
Gather a few rotten sticks to warm me.   20
OLD BANKS
Down with them when I bid thee, quickly; I'll make thy
bones rattle in thy skin else.
SAWYER
You won't, churl, cut-throat, miser. [*Throws down sticks*]
There they be. Would they stuck 'cross thy throat,
Thy bowels, thy maw, thy midriff.   25
OLD BANKS
Sayest thou me so? Hag, out of my ground. [*Hits her*]

---

cattell. And do now further confess, that I was the cause of those two nurse-
childrens death' (sig. C2)

17 *witch* Old Banks is speaking colloquially, not literally. In England (unlike the
Continent), Thomas writes, 'Most accusations of witchcraft related to supposed
maleficium and did not suggest that the accused person had contemplated even
a mental transfer of allegiance to the Devil' (p. 627)

18 *worse ... name* 'The conflict between resentment and a sense of obligation produced the ambivalence which made it possible for men to turn begging women
brusquely from the door, and yet suffer torments of conscience after having done
so. This ensuing guilt was fertile ground for witchcraft accusations ... and it
should be emphasised that these conflicts were not between the very rich and the
very poor, but between fairly poor and very poor' (Thomas, p. 673)

19 *makest thou upon* brings you to

20–2 (prose Q)
Gather ... else The discrepancy between Mother Sawyer's minimal needs and
Old Banks' severe punishment creates immediate sympathy for her and confirms
her view of events in her opening soliloquy

23 *You ... miser* Resorting to curses as Mother Sawyer does here was commonly
taken as proof of witchcraft
churl villain

25 *maw* belly

26 *Hag* (1) an evil spirit or daemon; (2) a witch; (3) an ugly old woman

SAWYER
Dost strike me, slave? Curmudgeon,
Now thy bones aches, thy joints cramps, and
Convulsions stretch and crack thy sinews!
OLD BANKS
Cursing, thou hag! Take that, and that.   30

[Strikes her and] exit

SAWYER
Strike, do, and withered may that hand and arm
Whose blows have lamed me, drop from the rotten trunk.
Abuse me! Beat me! Call me hag and witch!
What is the name? Where and by what art learned?
What spells, what charms, or invocations?
May the thing called Familiar be purchased?   35

Enter YOUNG [CUDDY] BANKS, *and three or four more*

YOUNG BANKS
A new head for the tabor, and silver tipping for the pipe.
Remember that, and forget not five leash of new bells.
FIRST DANCER
Double bells. Crooked Lane, ye shall have 'em straight in
Crooked Lane. Double bells all, if it be possible.   40

28–9 *Now ... sinews* Mother Sawyer's initial retort has now been transformed into
a full curse, displaying the social construction of witches; Dog is thus a natural
consequence when he appears and can be interpreted as a self-projection of guilt
(cf. Susan to Frank, IV.ii.s.d.69)

36 *Familiar* Technical term for the demonic companion of a witch, often in the form
of an animal; this belief was largely exclusive to English and Scottish accounts of
witchcraft

s.d. *YOUNG BANKS* The author William Rowley probably played (and wrote)
the part of Cuddy since he normally took clown roles, beginning in 1609; some
of his dialogue may first have begun in extemporaneous remarks or actions that
were successful in performance

37 *tabor* small drum

38 *leash* set of three

bells Morris dancers made (and still make) music by dancing vigorously while
wearing bells strapped around their legs; this was common entertainment

39 *Double* bass

40 *Crooked Lane* (speech prefix Q) A street near London Bridge that ran from New
Fish Street to St Michael's Lane, with the Black Bell, an inn, at one end. The
playwrights clearly know London in more intimate detail than they know
Edmonton

YOUNG BANKS
　　Double bells? Double coxcombs; trebles: buy me trebles, all
　　trebles: for our purpose is to be in the altitudes.

SECOND DANCER
　　All trebles? Not a mean?

YOUNG BANKS
　　Not one. The morris is so cast we'll have neither mean nor
　　base in our company, fellow Rowland.　　　　　　　　　　45

THIRD DANCER
　　What? Not a counter?

YOUNG BANKS
　　By no means, no hunting counter; leave that to Enville
　　Chase men. All trebles, all in the altitudes. Now for the dis-
　　posing of parts in the morris, little or no labour will serve.

SECOND DANCER
　　If you that be minded to follow your leader, know me, an　　50
　　ancient honour belonging to our house, for a fore-horse
　　team, and fore-gallant in a morris. My father's stable is not
　　unfurnished.

THIRD DANCER
　　So much for the fore-horse. But how for a good hobby-
　　horse?　　　　　　　　　　　　　　　　　　　　　　　55

YOUNG BANKS
　　For a hobby-horse? Let me see an almanac. [*Reads*

41　*coxcombs* fools (from the hat shaped like a cock's comb worn by jesters and pro-
　　fessional fools)
　　trebles voices or instruments highest in pitch
42　*altitudes* high notes
43　*mean* Intermediate range of sound; cf. Cuddy's pun in the following line
44　*morris* A round dance that takes its name from the homonym 'Moorish', since
　　originally the dancers blackened their faces
45　*fellow Rowland* Presumably the second dancer. The name may be a slip of the
　　pen, referring to Rowland Doyle, an actor in the King's Men's company
46　*counter* counter-tenor
47　*hunting counter* a hunting term for chasing the trail in the opposite direction
　　from the quarry
47–8　*Enville Chase* a royal hunting preserve (also known as Enfield Chase) then 12
　　miles north of London stocked by Elizabeth I and James I
51　*fore-horse* lead horse in a team
52　*fore-gallant* chief performer
53　*unfurnished* ill-equipped
54–5　*hobby-horse* one dancer was costumed as an especially high-spirited horse
　　with a light frame about his waist; he walked and pranced carrying the framed
　　costume. Cuddy thinks this is a most desirable part
56　*almanac* an annual book of astrological predictions

almanac] Midsummer-moon, let me see ye. When the moon's in the full, then's wit in the wane. No more. Use your best skill. Your morris will suffer an eclipse.

FIRST DANCER
    An eclipse?   60

YOUNG BANKS
    A strange one.

SECOND DANCER
    Strange?

YOUNG BANKS
    Yes, and most sudden. Remember the fore-gallant, and forget the hobby-horse. The whole body of your morris will be darkened. There be of us – but 'tis no matter. Forget the   65 hobby-horse.

FIRST DANCER
    Cuddy Banks, have you forgot since he paced it from Enville Chase to Edmonton? Cuddy, honest Cuddy, cast thy stuff.

YOUNG BANKS
    Suffer may ye all. It shall be known, I can take mine ease as   70 well as another man. Seek your hobby-horse where you can get him.

FIRST DANCER
    Cuddy, honest Cuddy, we confess, and are sorry for our neglect.

SECOND DANCER
    The old horse shall have a new bridle.   75

THIRD DANCER
    The caparisons new painted.

FOURTH DANCER
    The tail repaired.

---

57 *Midsummer* 29 June, a time of madness or strangeness; cf. proverb 'it is mid-summer moon with you' (M1117) and Shakespeare's use of the idea in *A Midsummer Night's Dream* and *Twelfth Night*

57–8 *When ... wane* The passage in the almanac which Young Banks quotes is proverbial (W555)

65–6 *Forget the hobby-horse* The allusion is to the phrase 'The hobby-horse is forgot', from a popular ballad on the Puritan's condemnation of morris dancing. Cf. *Love's Labour's Lost* III.i.129; *Hamlet* III.ii.135. There was a period when the hobby-horse was omitted from games played on May Day

68–9 *cast thy stuff* don't be that way; stop being moody

76 *caparisons* Coverings for the horse

FIRST DANCER
   The snaffle and the bosses new saffroned o'er. Kind:
SECOND DANCER
   Honest:
THIRD DANCER
   Loving, ingenious: 80
FOURTH DANCER
   Affable Cuddy.
YOUNG BANKS
   To show I am not flint, but affable, as you say, very well
   stuffed, a kind of warm dough or puff-paste, I relent, I con-
   nive, most affable Jack. Let the hobby-horse provide a
   strong back, he shall not want a belly when I am in 'em. But   85
   'uds me, Mother Sawyer.
FIRST DANCER
   The old Witch of Edmonton. If our mirth be not crossed –
SECOND DANCER
   Bless us, Cuddy, and let her curse her t'other eye out. What
   dost now?
YOUNG BANKS
   Ungirt, unblessed, says the proverb. But my girdle shall   90
   serve a riding knot. And a fig for all the witches in
   Christendom. What wouldst thou?
FIRST DANCER
   The devil cannot abide to be crossed.

78 *snaffle and the bosses* A bit with studs on each side
   saffroned Dyed orange
82 *flint* hard, unforgiving
83 *puff-paste* Light and flaky flour paste that has been heavily pounded
85 *want* lack
86 *'uds me* Slang abbreviation for 'God save me'
88 *t'other eye* Mother Sawyer had only one eye. Goodcole records this examination:
   'Quest[ion]. *How came your eye to be put out? Answ[er].* With a stick which one
   of my children had in the hand, that night my mother did dye it was done; for I
   was stooping by the bed side, and I by chance did hit my eye on the sharpe end
   of the sticke' (sig. D1). Similar deformities were often seen as a mark of witches;
   see Harris, p. 55
90 *Ungirt* unbelted; proverbial, U10   *girdle* belt
91 *riding knot* A running knot used for making nooses and snares
   knot (knit Q)
   a fig for A phrase of contempt; Cuddy pretends not to be frightened when pulling
   off his belt to defend himself from the witch
93 *crossed* opposed; this alludes to the popular belief that to cross the Devil's path
   will lead to harm from him; it may also allude to the protection from the Devil
   by carrying or brandishing a cross; cf. *Hamlet* I.i.127

SECOND DANCER
And scorns to come at any man's whistle.
THIRD DANCER
Away –   95
FOURTH DANCER
With the witch.
ALL
Away with the Witch of Edmonton.

> *Ex*[*eunt*] *in strange postur*[*es*]

SAWYER
Still vexed? Still tortured? That curmudgeon Banks
Is ground of all my scandal. I am shunned
And hated like a sickness. Made a scorn   100
To all degrees and sexes. I have heard old beldams
Talk of familiars in the shape of mice,
Rats, ferrets, weasels and I wot not what,
That have appeared, and sucked, some say, their blood.
But by what means they came acquainted with them,   105
I'm now ignorant. Would some power good or bad
Instruct me which way I might be revenged
Upon this churl, I'd go out of myself,

---

97 s.d. *strange postures* Cuddy and the dancers have either been affected by Mother
Sawyer or the Devil or else assume such postures in an attempt to protect themselves

99 *scandal* embarrassment; false charges

101 *degrees* social classes
beldams hags

103 *wot* know

104 *sucked* According to popular belief, witches fed their familiars with their blood
either by scratching themselves or allowing the familiar to suck blood from
them, raising the skin and marking it with the 'witch's mark' so that what
remained resembled a teat. Goodcole notes of witnesses, 'And they all three said,
that they a little above the Fundiment [anus] of *Elizabeth Sawyer* the prisoner,
there indited before the Bench for a Witch, found a thing like a Teate the bignesse of the little finger, and the length of halfe a finger, which was branched at
the top like a teate, and seemed as though one had suckt it, and that the bottome
thereof was blew, and the top of it was redd' (sig. B3v). The Witchcraft Act of
1604 refers to the feeding of familiars, for which see Thomas, p. 530. Mother
Sawyer testified, 'The place where the Diuell suckt my bloud was a little above
my fundiment, and that place chosen by himselfe; and in that place chosen by
himself by continuall drawing, there is a thing in the forme of a Teate, at which
the diuell would sucke mee. And I asked the Diuell why hee would sucke my
bloud, and hee sayd it was to nourish him' (sigs. C3–C3v); cf. Harris, pp. 21–2

And give this fury leave to dwell within
This ruined cottage, ready to fall with age.　　　　　110
Abjure all goodness. Be at hate with prayer,
And study curses, imprecations,
Blasphemous speeches, oaths, detested oaths,
Or anything that's ill; so I might work
Revenge upon this miser, this black cur,　　　　　115
That barks and bites, and sucks the very blood
Of me, and of my credit. 'Tis all one,
To be a witch as to be counted one.
Vengeance, shame, ruin, light upon that canker.

Enter DOG

DOG
　　Ho! Have I found thee cursing? Now thou art mine own.　　120
SAWYER
　　Thine? What art thou?
DOG　　　　　　　　　　　　He thou hast so often importuned
　　To appear to thee, the Devil.
SAWYER　　　　　　　　　　　Bless me! The Devil?

110　*This ruined cottage* Mother Sawyer is referring to her body
117　*credit* reputation
119　s.d. *Enter* DOG A dog was a conventional familiar and the choices available
　　　(dog, cat, spider, toad) may have been the easiest (and most visible) to stage; cf.
　　　Goodcole: '*Question.* In what shape would the Diuell come vnto you? *Answere.*
　　　Alwayes in the shape of a dogge, and of two collars, sometimes of blacke and
　　　sometimes of white' (sig. C2v). Hoy argues that the audience must decide if Dog
　　　is the Devil or can be Mother Sawyer's overwrought imagination (III, 238) but
　　　the actual appearance and dialogue of Dog on stage might more strongly support
　　　the former
120　*cursing* So Goodcole's *Wonderful Discouerie*: '*Question.* By what meanes came
　　　*you to haue acquaintance with the Diuell, and when was the first time that you
　　　saw him, and how did you know that it was the Diuell? Answere.* The first time
　　　that the Diuell came vnto me was, when I was cursing, swearing and blasphem-
　　　ing; he then rushed in vpon me, and neuer before that time did I see him, or he
　　　me; and when he, namely the Diuel, came to me, the first words that hee spake
　　　vnto me were these: *Oh! haue I now found you cursing, swearing, and blas-
　　　pheming? now you are mine*' (sigs. C1–C1v). James I noted in his *Daemonologie*
　　　(1597; 1603) that desperate persons calling on the Devil often met him in fam-
　　　iliar shapes
121　*importuned* pleaded with
122　*appear* Thomas remarks that contemporary religion emphasized the continual
　　　presence of the Devil and his agents (pp. 638ff.)

DOG
    Come, do not fear, I love thee much too well
    To hurt or fright thee. If I seem terrible,
    It is to such as hate me. I have found   125
    Thy love unfeigned; have seen and pitied
    Thy open wrongs, and come out of my love
    To give thee just revenge against thy foes.
SAWYER
    May I believe thee?
DOG   To confirm't, command me
    Do any mischief unto man or beast,   130
    And I'll effect it, on condition,
    That uncompelled thou make a deed of gift
    Of soul and body to me.
SAWYER   Out, alas!

123 *do not fear* Thus Goodcole: '*Question. What sayd you to the Diuell, when hee came vnto you and spake vnto you, were you not afraide of him? If you did feare him, what sayd the Diuell then vnto you? Answere.* I was in a very greate feare, when I saw the Diuell, but hee did bid me not to feare him at all, for hee would do me no hurt at all, but would do for mee whatsoeuer I should require of him, and as he promised vnto me, he alwayes did such mischiefes as I did bid him to do, both on the bodies of Christians and beastes: if I did bid him vexe them to death, as oftentimes I did so bid him, it was then presently by him so done' (sigs. C1v–C2)

127 *out of my love* Dog gains power over Mother Sawyer by offering her the only love (and pity) she knows. 'These creatures may have been the only friends these lonely old women possessed' (Thomas, p. 626)

132–5 *make a deed ... seal it with thy blood* Cf. Goodcole: '*Question.* What talke had the Diuel and you together, when that he appeared to you, and what did he aske of you, and what did you desire of him? *Answere.* He asked of me, when hee came vnto me, how I did, and what he should doe for mee, and demanded of mee my soule and body; threatning then to teare me in peeces, if that I did not grant vnto him my soule and my body which he asked of me. *Question. What did you after such the Diuells asking of you, to haue your Soule and Body, and after this his threatning of you, did you for feare grant vnto the Diuell his desire? Answer.* Yes, I granted for feare vnto the Diuell his request of my Soule and body; and to seale this my promise made vnto him, I then gaue him leaue to sucke of my bloud, the which hee asked of me' (sigs. C2v–C3)

132 *deed of gift* Mother Sawyer seems to sign over her soul here to Dog as the Devil despite a common belief that no person could so easily undo baptismal rites. In *A Discourse of the Damned Art of Witchcraft* (1608) William Perkins writes that 'consenting to use the help of the devil, either by open or secret league, wittingly and willingly: wherein standeth the very thing that maketh a witch to be a witch, the yielding of consent upon covenant'

My soul and body?
DOG   And that instantly,
    And seal it with thy blood. If thou deniest,   135
    I'll tear thy body in a thousand pieces.
SAWYER
    I know not where to seek relief. But shall I
    After such covenants sealed, see full revenge
    On all that wrong me?
DOG   Ha, ha, silly woman!
    The Devil is no liar to such as he loves.   140
    Didst ever know or hear the Devil a liar
    To such as he affects?
SAWYER   Then I am thine, at least
    So much of me as I can call mine own.
DOG   Equivocations?
    Art mine or no? Speak, or I'll tear –
SAWYER   All thine.
DOG
    Seal't with thy blood.

                  Sucks her arm, thunder and lightning

                            See, now I dare call thee mine;   145
    For proof, command me. Instantly I'll run
    To any mischief, goodness can I none.
SAWYER
    And I desire as little. There's an old churl,
    One Banks –
DOG   That wronged thee.
    He lamed thee, called thee witch.   150
SAWYER
    The same. First upon him I'd be revenged.
DOG
    Thou shalt. Do but name how.
SAWYER   Go, touch his life.
DOG
    I cannot.

---

136 *tear thy body* Mother Sawyer does not agree to make a pact with Dog until he
    threatens her with bodily harm
145 s.d. *Sucks her arm* Mother Sawyer must draw blood to seal their pact; in the
    1981 RSC production she produced blood by scratching her chest
150 *lamed thee* Dog confirms Mother Sawyer's sense of herself as the victim of Old
    Banks especially
152 *touch his life* kill him
153 *cannot* Thomas notes that common belief held the Devil was powerless before
    virtue (p. 592)

SAWYER
  Hast thou not vowed? Go, kill the slave.
DOG
  I wonnot.   155
SAWYER
  I'll cancel then my gift.
DOG   Ha, ha!
SAWYER   Dost laugh?
  Why wilt not kill him?
DOG   Fool, because I cannot.
  Though we have power, know, it is circumscribed,
  And tied in limits. Though he be cursed to thee,
  Yet of himself he is loving to the world,   160
  And charitable to the poor. Now men
  That, as he, love goodness, though in smallest measure,
  Live without compass of our reach. His cattle
  And corn I'll kill and mildew. But his life,
  (Until I take him as I late found thee,   165
  Cursing and swearing) I have no power to touch.
SAWYER
  Work on his corn and cattle then.
DOG   I shall.
  The Witch of Edmonton shall see his fall.
  If she at least put credit in my power,
  And in mine only; make orisons to me,   170
  And none but me.
SAWYER   Say how, and in what manner?
DOG
  I'll tell thee, when thou wishest ill;
  Corn, man or beast, would spoil or kill,
  Turn thy back against the sun,
  And mumble this short orison: 175

155 *wonnot* (1) don't know how; (2) I will not

156 *cancel ... gift* Despite Dog's accusation of Old Banks' persecution of Mother
    Sawyer, he will not grant her the one wish for which she agreed to the pact with
    him; she is thus (despite her 'virtue') in a dilemma similar to Frank's when he
    consents to marry Susan. Both have made mistaken moral choices and commit-
    ments for understandable reasons

159 *cursed* evil

163 *without compass of* beyond

166 *touch* harm

170 *orisons* prayers

175–83 *orison ... Speak Latin* Thus Goodcole's account of Mother Sawyer's exam-
    ination: '*Quest. Did the Diuell at any time find you praying when he came vnto
    you, and did not the Diuell forbid you to pray to Iesus Christ, but to him alone?*

If thou to death or shame pursue 'em,
Sanctibicetur nomen tuum.

SAWYER
If thou to death or shame pursue 'em,
Sanctibecetur nomen tuum.

DOG
Perfect. Farewell. Our first-made promises   180
We'll put in execution against Banks.   *Exit*

SAWYER
Contaminetur nomen tuum. I'm an expert scholar;
Speak Latin, or I know not well what language,
As well as the best of 'em.

Enter YOUNG BANKS

But who comes here?   185
The son of my worst foe. *To death pursue 'em,*
Et sanctabecetur nomen tuum.

YOUNG BANKS
What's that she mumbles? The Devil's *pater noster*? Would
it were else. Mother Sawyer, good morrow.

SAWYER
Ill morrow to thee, and all the world,   190
That flout a poor old woman.

---

and did not he bid you pray to him the Divell, as he taught you? Answ. Yes, he
found me once praying, and he asked of me to whom I prayed, and I answered
him, to Iesus Christ; and he charged me then to pray no more to Iesus Christ, but
to him the Diuell, and he the Diuell taught me this prayer, *Sanctibicetur nomen*
tuum. Amen. *Quest. Were you euer taught these Latine words before by any*
person else, or did you euer heare it before of anybody, or can you say more of
it? Answ. No, I was not taught it by any body else, but by the Diuell alone;
neither doe I vnderstand the meaning of these words, nor can speake any more
Latine words' (sig. C4v)

177 *Sanctibicetur nomen tuum* In a parody of the phrase 'Hallowed be thy name'
   from the Lord's Prayer, *sanctibicetur* is substituted for *sanctificetur*; as the Devil,
   Dog is unable to teach the Lord's Prayer correctly

179 *Sanctibecetur* That Mother Sawyer instantly makes a mistake shows her ignor-
   ance (and perhaps a residual innocence) as well as the weak hold she has on the
   charm Dog has tried to teach her. Alternatively, it may be a sign of her damnation

180 *Perfect* Either Dog lies or he fails to notice his disciple's error

182 *Contaminetur ... scholar* In a further joke, Mother Sawyer uses a correct term
   (*contaminetur* means polluted or defiled) she has not been taught; this may continue to suggest residual grace or self-damnation

183 *Speak Latin* Knowledge of Latin was restricted to the educated classes and clergy

188 *pater noster* prayer (literally, 'Our Father', signifying the Lord's Prayer)

To death pursue 'em,
And *sanctabacetur nomen tuum.*

YOUNG BANKS
Nay, Good Gammer Sawyer, whate'er it please my father
to call you, I know you are –   195

SAWYER
A witch.

YOUNG BANKS
A witch? Would you were else i'faith.

SAWYER
Your father knows I am by this.

YOUNG BANKS
I would he did.

SAWYER
And so in time may you.   200

YOUNG BANKS
I would I might else. But witch or no witch, you are a
motherly woman. And though my father be a kind of God-
bless-us, as they say, I have an earnest suit to you; and if
you'll be so kind to ka me one good turn, I'll be so courteous as to kob you another.   205

SAWYER
What's that? To spurn, beat me,
And call me witch, as your
Kind father doth?

YOUNG BANKS
My father? I am ashamed to own him. If he has hurt the
head of thy credit, there's money to buy thee a plaster. 210
[*Gives her money*] And a small courtesy I would require at
thy hands.

SAWYER
You seem a good young man. [*Aside*] And
I must dissemble, the better to accomplish

194 *Gammer* Grandmother (a term of familiarity)
198 *by this* by this time; Mother Sawyer assumes that by now Dog will have seen to
    Old Banks
201–2 *you ... woman* Ironically, Young Banks gives Mother Sawyer more unso-
    licited respect than she received from soliciting the help of Dog; cf. Winifred's
    sympathy for Frank in Act IV
202–3 *God-bless-us* religious man
203 *suit* request (indicating respect)
203–5 *if ... another* Proverbial for mutual help; cf. 'scratch my back and I'll scratch
    yours' (K1)
204 *ka* give
205 *kob* give

My revenge. [*To him*] But for this silver,   215
What wouldst have me do? Bewitch thee?

YOUNG BANKS

No, by no means; I am bewitched already. I would have
thee so good as to unwitch me, or witch another with me
for company.

SAWYER

I understand thee not. Be plain, my son.   220

YOUNG BANKS

As a pike-staff, Mother. You know Kate Carter.

SAWYER

The wealthy yeoman's daughter. What of her?

YOUNG BANKS

That same party has bewitched me.

SAWYER

Bewitched thee?

YOUNG BANKS

Bewitched me, *hisce auribus*. I saw a little Devil fly out of   225
her eye like a burbolt, which sticks at this hour up to the
feathers in my heart. Now my request is to send one of thy
what-d'ye-call-'ems, either to pluck that out, or stick
another as fast in hers. Do, and here's my hand, I am thine
for three lives.   230

SAWYER

[*Aside*] We shall have sport. [*To him*] Thou art
In love with her?

YOUNG BANKS

Up to the very hilts, Mother.

SAWYER

And thou'dst have me make her love thee too.

YOUNG BANKS

[*Aside*] I think she'll prove a witch in earnest. [*To her*] Yes,   235
I could find in my heart to strike her three quarters deep in
love with me too.

---

221 *pike-staff* straight walking-stick; proverbial (P322)

223 *bewitched me* This line, which anticipates Young Banks' sight of Katherine's
Spirit created by Dog (III.i.s.d.73), has particular force for Mother Sawyer

225 *hisce auribus* 'in these very ears' (Latin)

226 *burbolt* blunt-headed arrow for hunting birds

230 *for three lives* Allusion to the law concerning property held for three generations

233 *hilts* handles (of swords and daggers)

234 *And ... too* Mother Sawyer's unconscious echo of Dog here signals her servitude
to him

SAWYER

But dost thou think that I can do't,
And I alone?

YOUNG BANKS

Truly, Mother Witch, I do verily believe so. And when I see   240
it done, I shall be half persuaded so too.

SAWYER

It's enough. What art can do, be sure of.
Turn to the west, and whatso'er thou hearest or seest,
Stand silent, and be not afraid.

> *She stamps. Enter the* DOG; *he fawns and leaps*
> *upon her*

YOUNG BANKS

Afraid, Mother Witch? Turn my face to the west? [*Aside*] I   245
said I should always have a back-friend of her; and now it's
out. And her little Devil should be hungry, come sneaking
behind me, like a cowardly catchpole, and clap his talons
on my haunches. 'Tis woundy cold sure. I dudder and
shake like an aspen-leaf every joint of me.   250

SAWYER

To scandal and disgrace pursue 'em,
Et sanctabicetur nomen tuum.
How now, my son, how is't?

> *Exit* DOG

YOUNG BANKS

Scarce in a clean life, Mother Witch. But did your goblin
and you spout Latin together?   255

SAWYER

A kind of charm I work by. Didst thou hear me?

---

244 s.d. *She stamps* According to the Witchcraft Statute of 1604, the invocation of
    evil spirits was a felony; at this point, Mother Sawyer is being identified as a
    criminal (the law was in effect until 1736)
246 *back-friend* supporter, ally
247 *out* occurred
    And suppose
248 *catchpole* constable or sergeant (with pun on 'back-friend')
249 *woundy* excessively
    dudder shiver
250 *aspen-leaf* Proverbial; L140
256 *charm* That Mother Sawyer uses Dog's power against kindly Young Banks
    shows both her desperation and her self-condemnation; she has acted the part of
    a witch for ridiculously low stakes

YOUNG BANKS

I heard I know not the Devil what mumble in a scurvy base
tone, like a drum that had taken cold in the head the last
muster. Very comfortable words. What were they? And
who taught them you?   260

SAWYER

A great learned man.

YOUNG BANKS

Learned man? Learned Devil it was as soon? But what?
What comfortable news about the party?

SAWYER

Who? Kate Carter? I'll tell thee,
Thou knowst the stile at the west end   265
Of thy father's peas-field. Be there
Tomorrow night after sunset;
And the first live thing thou seest,
Be sure to follow, and that
Shall bring thee to thy love.   270

YOUNG BANKS

In the peas-field? Has she a mind to codlings already? The
first living thing I meet, you say, shall bring me to her?

SAWYER

To a sight of her, I mean. She will seem
Wantonly coy, and flee thee. But
Follow her close, and boldly.   275
Do but embrace her in thy arms
Once, and she is thine own.

YOUNG BANKS

At the stile, at the west end of my father's peas-land, the
first live thing I see, follow and embrace her, and she shall
be thine. Nay, and I come to embracing once, she shall be   280
mine; I'll go near to make at eaglet else.   *Exit*

SAWYER

A ball well bandied. Now the set's half won.
The father's wrong I'll wreak upon the son.   *Exit*

---

258 *cold ... head* Young Banks cannot avoid a pun; it is the parallel characteristic to
    Old Carter's proverbs
259 *muster* calling of troops
262 *soon* likely
271 *codlings* peas (with a pun on codpiece that covers the scrotum in man's dress)
281 *at eaglet* act as amateur (the eaglet was trained by its parent before acting on its
    own)
282 *bandied* thrown to and fro
    set a fixed number of games (as in tennis)

Act II, Scene ii

Enter [OLD] CARTER, WARBECK, SOMERTON

OLD CARTER
How now, gentlemen, cloudy? I know, Master Warbeck,
you are in a fog about my daughter's marriage.
WARBECK
And can you blame me, sir?
OLD CARTER
Nor you me justly. Wedding and hanging are tied up both
in a proverb, and destiny is the juggler that unties the knot.   5
My hope is, you are reserved to a richer fortune than my
poor daughter.
WARBECK
However, your promise –
OLD CARTER
Is a kind of debt, I confess it.
WARBECK
Which honest men should pay.   10
OLD CARTER
Yet some gentlemen break in that point, now and then, by
your leave, sir.
SOMERTON
I confess thou hast had a little wrong
In the wench. But patience is the only salve
To cure it. Since Thorney has won the wench,   15
He has most reason to wear her.
WARBECK
Love in this kind admits no reason to wear her.
OLD CARTER
Then love's a fool, and what wise man will take exception?
SOMERTON
Come, frolic. Ned, were every man master
Of his own fortune, Fate might pick straws,   20
And Destiny go a-wool-gathering.

---

1 *cloudy* troubled
5 *proverb* 'Wedding and hanging go by destiny' (W232); another forewarning
8 *promise* – (promise. Q)
8–9 *promise … debt* Proverbial; P603
19 *frolic* carefree
20 *pick straws* become tired
21 *a-wool-gathering* absent-minded

WARBECK
You hold yours in a string, though.
'Tis well. But if there be any equity,
Look thou to meet the like usage ere long.
SOMERTON
In my love to her sister Katherine? Indeed,   25
They are a pair of arrows drawn out of one quiver,
And should fly at an even length, if she do run
After her sister.
WARBECK   Look for the same mercy
At my hands, as I have received at thine.
SOMERTON
She'll keep a surer compass. I have   30
Too strong a confidence to mistrust her.
WARBECK
And that confidence is a wind,
That has blown many a married man ashore at Cuckold's
    Haven,
I can tell you. I wish yours more prosperous though.
OLD CARTER
Whate'er you wish, I'll master my promise to him.   35
WARBECK
Yes, as you did to me.
OLD CARTER
No more of that, if you love me. But for the more assur-
ance, the next offered occasion shall consummate the
marriage. And that once sealed—

Enter YOUNG [FRANK] THORNEY *and* SUSAN

---

22 *hold ... string* be in absolute control (from the proverb 'hold the world on a
   string', W886)
27 *run* take
30 *compass* (1) measure (from space denoted by the markings of a compass); (2)
   direction (compass-wise meant going steadily to the mark)
33 *Cuckold's Haven* Land along the Kent/south side of the Thames about a mile
   below Rotherhithe Church said to have been granted by King John to a man in
   recompense for having seduced his wife, a tale commemorated by an Eastcheap
   butcher on St Luke's Day, 18 October, by erecting a pair of horns on a pole there
   (see *Eastward Ho!* IV.i); also, more generally, a place of safety or refuge
35 *master* keep

SOMERTON
    Leave the manage of the rest to my care.   40
    But see, the bridegroom and bride comes;
    The new pair of Sheffield knives fitted both
    To one sheath.
WARBECK   The sheath might have been better fitted,
    If somebody had their due. But –
SOMERTON
    No harsh language, if thou lovest me.   45
    Frank Thorney has done –
WARBECK
    No more than I, or thou, or any man,
    Things so standing, would have attempted.
SOMERTON
    Good morrow, Master Bridegroom.
WARBECK
    Come, give thee joy. Mayst thou live   50
    Long and happy in thy fair choice.
FRANK
    I thank ye gentlemen. Kind Master Warbeck,
    I find you loving.
WARBECK   Thorney, that creature,
    [*Aside*] (much good do thee with her)
    [*To him*] Virtue and beauty hold fair mixture in her.   55
    She's rich no doubt, in both. Yet were she fairer,
    Thou art right worthy of her. Love her, Thorney,
    'Tis nobleness in thee, in her but duty.
    The match is fair and equal. The success
    I leave to censure. Farewell, Mistress Bride: 60
    Till now elected, thy old scorn deride.   *Exit*
SOMERTON
    Good, Master Thorney.   [*Exit*]

42–3 *Sheffield knives ... one sheath* (1) A traditional emblem for marriage (as two
    made one); (2) a customary wedding present, Sheffield having a reputation for
    producing especially fine knives
45–6 *No ... done* Q assigns these lines to Old Carter, but *thou* would be an inap-
    propriate word for one of his class
  60 *censure* That is, censure opinions (of others)

OLD CARTER
    Nay, you shall not part till you see the barrels run a-tilt,
    gentlemen.   *Exit*
SUSAN
    Why change you your face, sweetheart?
FRANK   Who? I?   65
    For nothing.
SUSAN   Dear, say not so. A spirit of your
    Constancy cannot endure this change for nothing.
    I have observed strange variations in you.
FRANK   In me?
SUSAN
    In you, sir. Awake, you seem to dream,
    And in your sleep you utter sudden and   70
    Distracted accents, like one at enmity
    With peace. Dear loving husband, if I may dare
    To challenge any interest in you,
    Give me the reason fully. You may trust
    My breast as safely as your own.
FRANK   With what?   75
    You half amaze me, prithee.
SUSAN   Come, you shall not;
    Indeed, you shall not shut me from partaking
    The least dislike that grieves you. I am all yours.
FRANK
    And I all thine.
SUSAN   You are not, if you keep
    The least grief from me. But I find the cause;   80
    It grew from me.
FRANK   From you?
SUSAN   From some distaste
    In me or my behaviour. You are not kind
    In the concealment. 'Las, sir, I am young,
    Silly and plain; more, strange to those contents
    A wife should offer. Say but in what I fail,   85
    I'll study satisfaction.
FRANK   Come, in nothing.
SUSAN
    I know I do. Knew I as well in what,

---

63 *barrels run a-tilt* A tilting contest using spears aimed at barrels, here made a wed-
    ding festivity; by tradition, this was a skilled match used by burgesses and
    yeomen who were barred as combatants in jousts and tournaments since they
    were not of sufficiently high rank (esquire)
71 *accents* words
86 *study* learn

You should not long be sullen. Prithee love,
If I have been immodest or too bold,
Speak't in a frown. If peevishly too nice,   90
Show't in a smile. Thy liking is the glass
By which I'll habit my behaviour.
FRANK
    Wherefore dost weep now?
SUSAN   You, sweet, have the power
To make me passionate as an April day.
Now smile, then weep, now pale, then crimson red.   95
You are the powerful moon of my blood's sea,
To make it ebb or flow into my face,
As your looks change.
FRANK   Change thy conceit, I prithee.
Thou art all perfection. Diana herself
Swells in thy thoughts, and moderates thy beauty.   100
Within thy left eye amorous Cupid sits
Feathering love-shafts, whose golden heads he dipped
– In thy chaste breast. In the other lies
Blushing Adonis scarfed in modesties.
And still as wanton Cupid blows love-fires,   105
Adonis quenches out unchaste desires.
And from these two I briefly do imply
A perfect emblem of thy modesty.
Then, prithee, dear, maintain no more dispute,
For when thou speakest, it's fit all tongues be mute.   110
SUSAN
    Come, come, those golden strings of flattery
Shall not tie up my speech, sir; I must know
The ground of your disturbance.
FRANK   Then look here;
For here, here is the fen in which this Hydra
Of discontent grows rank.
SUSAN   Heaven shield it. Where?   115

---

90   *nice* coy
98   *conceit* example; forceful idea
99   *Diana* As goddess of chastity
101 *Cupid* The child-god of love whose golden arrows caused love and whose lead
     arrows repelled it
104 *Adonis* Exemplary of beauty; he attracted Venus
     scarfed clothed
114 *fen* marshy ground
     Hydra The many-headed beast that according to myth grew back two snake
     heads for every one cut off

FRANK
    In mine own bosom. Here the cause has root;
    The poisoned leeches twist about my heart,
    And will, I hope, confound me.
SUSAN   You speak riddles.
FRANK
    Take't plainly then. 'Twas told me by a woman
    Known and approved in palmistry,   120
    I should have two wives.
SUSAN   Two wives? Sir, I take it
    Exceeding likely. But let not conceit hurt you.
    You are afraid to bury me?
FRANK   No, no, my Winifred.
SUSAN
    How say you? Winifred? You forget me.
FRANK
    No, I forget myself, Susan.
SUSAN   In what?   125
FRANK
    Talking of wives, I pretend Winifred,
    A maid that at my mother's waited on me
    Before thyself.
SUSAN   I hope, sir, she may live
    To take my place. But why should all this move you?
FRANK
    [Aside] The poor girl, she has't before thee,   130
    And that's the fiend torments me.
SUSAN   Yet why should this
    Raise mutiny within you? Such presages
    Prove often false. Or say it should be true?

117 *leeches* Worms used in medicine to suck bad blood from the sick

118 *confound* undo, ruin

119–21 *woman ... wives* Frank associates himself with palmistry, a pseudo-science
    not unrelated to witchcraft

122 *likely* That is, unlikely; Susan is mocking Frank

126 *pretend* (1) lay claim to; (2) use as a pretext
    Winifred Ambiguous; (1) a slip of the tongue, suggesting an unexpected act of
    conscience; (2) an attempt to confess – the virtue Frank earlier claimed for him-
    self (I.ii.197)

130 *poor girl* The Revels editor thinks Susan deciphers this as a reference to the
    former wife's death, but the context implies she is thinking of other future wives;
    either way, Susan is shown as ignorant of the real situation despite the slip of
    Frank's tongue. Q does not make this speech an aside
    has't That is, has my marriage vow

FRANK
  That I should have another wife?
SUSAN   Yes, many;
  If they be good, the better.
FRANK   Never any equal   135
  To thee in goodness.
SUSAN   Sir, I could wish I were
  Much better for you; yet if I knew your fate
  Ordained you for another, I could wish
  (So well I love you and your hopeful pleasure)
  Me in my grave, and my poor virtues added   140
  To my successor.
FRANK   Prithee, prithee, talk not
  Of death or graves; thou art so rare a goodness,
  As death would rather put itself to death
  Than murder thee. But we, as all things else,
  Are mutable and changing.
SUSAN   Yet you still move   145
  In your first sphere of discontent. Sweet, chase
  Those clouds of sorrow, and shine clearly on me.
FRANK
  At my return I will.
SUSAN   Return? Ah me!
  Will you then leave me?
FRANK   For a time I must.
  But how? As birds their young, or loving bees   150
  Their hives, to fetch home richer dainties.
SUSAN   Leave me?
  Now has my fear met its effect. You shall not,
  Cost it my life, you shall not.
FRANK   Why? Your reason?
SUSAN
  Like to the lapwing have you all this while
  With your false love deluded me? Pretending   155
  Counterfeit senses for your discontent,
  And now at last it is by chance stole from you.

---

134 *That ... wife?* Frank is recalling the falsely claimed prophecy that he will have
   two wives
   Yes, many Susan has innocently hit upon the truth, her intuition meeting his suddenly guilty conscience
140 *Me in my grave* Another ironic anticipation; cf. 153 below
152 *met its effect* come to pass
154 *lapwing* A bird known for decoying intruders away from its nest; proverbial
   (L68)

FRANK
  What? What by chance?
SUSAN   Your pre-appointed meeting
  Of single combat with young Warbeck.
FRANK   Ha!
SUSAN
  Even so. Dissemble not, 'tis too apparent.   160
  Then in his look I read it. Deny it not;
  I see't apparent. Cost it my undoing,
  And unto that my life, I will not leave you.
FRANK
  Not until when?
SUSAN   Till he and you be friends.
  Was this your cunning? and then flam me off   165
  With an old witch, two wives, and Winifred?
  You're not so kind indeed as I imagined.
FRANK
  And you more fond by far than I expected.
  It is a virtue that attends thy kind.
  But of our business within. And by this kiss   170
  I'll anger thee no more; troth chuck I will not.

                        [*Kisses her*]

SUSAN
  You shall have no just cause.
FRANK   Dear Sue, I shall not.

                                        Exeunt

Act III, Scene i

Enter CUDDY BANKS *and Morris dancers*

FIRST DANCER
  Nay, Cuddy, prithee do not leave us now. If we part all this
  night, we shall not meet before day.
SECOND DANCER
  I prithee, Banks, let's keep together now.

163 *unto that* even
165 *flam* Trick by distracting
168 *fond* Perhaps deliberately ambiguous, answering Frank's divided conscience, as
      'loving' and 'foolish' (both in reference to Susan)
171 *troth* Elision of 'by my truth', a common pledge
      chuck A common term of affection

YOUNG BANKS

If you were wise, a word would serve. But as you are, I
must be forced to tell you again, I have a little private busi-   5
ness, an hour's work; it may prove but an half hour's, as
luck may serve; and then I take horse and along with you.
Have we e'er a witch in the morris?

FIRST DANCER

No, no; no woman's part but Maid Marian, and the hobby-
horse.   10

YOUNG BANKS

I'll have a witch; I love a witch.

FIRST DANCER

Faith, witches themselves are so common now-a-days, that
the counterfeit will not be regarded. They say we have three
or four in Edmonton, besides Mother Sawyer.

SECOND DANCER

I would she would dance her part with us.   15

THIRD DANCER

So would not I, for, if she comes, the Devil and all comes
along with her.

YOUNG BANKS

Well, I'll have a witch. I have loved a witch ever since I
played at cherry-pit. Leave me, and get my horse dressed.
Give him oats; but water him not till I come. Whither do   20
we foot it first?

SECOND DANCER

To Sir Arthur Clarington's first, then whither thou wilt.

YOUNG BANKS

Well, I am content. But we must up to Carter's, the rich
yeoman. I must be seen on hobby-horse there.

---

4 *YOUNG BANKS* Q begins here to use the speech prefix 'Clow[n]' for Young
Banks

If ... serve Proverbial ('A word to the wise man is enough', W781)

7 *horse* hobby-horse (see note to II.i.54–5); it was sometimes associated with the
witch's broomstick and is therefore especially appropriate for Young Banks to
bring

8 *witch* Perhaps also a reference to Maid Marian, originally queen of the witch's
coven before becoming the companion of Robin Hood and frequently played by
a man in morris dances

19 *cherry-pit* A traditional children's game in which cherry stones were tossed into
a small hole

21 *foot it* (1) walk; (2) dance

FIRST DANCER

    O, I smell him now. I'll lay my ears Banks is in love, and   25
that's the reason he would walk melancholy by himself.

YOUNG BANKS

    Ha! Who was that said I was in love?

FIRST DANCER

    Not I.

SECOND DANCER

    Not I.

YOUNG BANKS

    Go to. No more of that. When I understand what you   30
speak, I know what you say. Believe that.

FIRST DANCER

    Well, 'twas I, I'll not deny it. I meant no hurt in't. I have
seen you walk up to Carter's of Chessum. Banks, were not
you there last Shrovetide?

YOUNG BANKS

    Yes, I was ten days together there the last Shrovetide.   35

SECOND DANCER

    How could that be, when there are but seven days in the
week?

YOUNG BANKS

    Prithee peace, I reckon *stila nova* as a traveller. Thou
understandest as a fresh-water farmer, that never sawest a
week beyond sea. Ask any soldier that ever received his pay   40
but in the Low Countries, and he'll tell thee there are eight
days in the week there, hard by. How dost thou think they
rise in High Germany, Italy, and those remoter places?

THIRD DANCER

    Ay, but simply there are but seven days in the week yet.

25 *smell him* know what he's up to
     lay bet
30 *Go to* go on with you (common expression)
33 *Chessum* Probably Cheshunt, Hertfordshire, then four miles north of Edmonton
34 *Shrovetide* The week before Lent, often marked by festivity
38 *stila nova* new style; a learned joke since the new Gregorian calendar introduced
     on the Continent in 1582, seven days ahead of the English calendar, was not
     adopted in England until 1752
39 *fresh-water* inexperienced (in analogy to a 'fresh-water sailor' who has never
     been to sea)
40–2 *soldier ... hard by* Time went slowly for ill-paid ('hard by') soldiers, hence
     weeks appear to have eight days
41 *Low Countries* the Netherlands (then 18 separate provinces)

YOUNG BANKS

No, simply as thou understandest. Prithee, look but in the   45
lover's almanac; when he has been but three days absent,
'Oh', says he, 'I have not seen my love these seven years.
There's a long cut.' When he comes to her again, and
embraces her, 'O', says he, 'now methinks I am in heaven';
and that's a pretty step. He that can get up to heaven in ten   50
days, need not repent his journey. You may ride a hundred
days in a caroche, and be further off than when you set
forth. But I pray you, good morris-mates, now leave me. I
will be with you by midnight.

FIRST DANCER

Well, since he will be alone, we'll back again, and trouble   55
him no more.

ALL

But remember, Banks.

YOUNG BANKS

The hobby-horse shall be remembered. But hark you. Get
Poldavis, the barber's boy, for the witch; because he can
show his art better than another.   60

                    Exeunt [*all but* YOUNG BANKS]

Well, now to my walk. I am near the place where I should
meet I know not what. Say I meet a thief, I must follow
him, if to the gallows. Say I meet a horse, or hare, or hound,
still I must follow; some slow-paced beast, I hope. Yet love
is full of lightness in the heaviest lovers.   65

                    [*Enter* DOG]

Ha! My guide is come. A water-dog. I am thy first man,
Sculler. I go with thee. Ply no other but myself. Away with

---

48 *cut* misfortune
52 *caroche* gentleman's coach
59 *Poldavis* Cf. Actors' Names, line 15. Hoy sees an allusion to poldavy, a coarse
    canvas used for sailcloth – hence clown, rustic or lower order of tradesman, a
    social slur (Hoy, III, 254)
62 *Say* suppose
65 *heaviest* (1) most serious; (2) overweight (as Young Banks' self-reference)
66 *water-dog* A dog, often a spaniel, taught by hunters to retrieve ducks and other
    waterbirds
67 *Sculler* oarsman (cf. line 72)
    Ply take as passenger

the boat. Land me but at Katherine's Dock, my sweet
Katherine's Dock, and I'll be a fare to thee. [DOG *leads*]
That way? Nay, which way thou wilt, thou knowst the way   70
better than I. [*Aside*] Fine gentle cur it is, and well brought
up, I warrant him. [*To* DOG] We go a-ducking, spaniel;
thou shalt fetch me the ducks, pretty kind rascal.

> *Enter* SPIRIT *in shape of* KATHERINE, *vizarded, and
> takes it off*

SPIRIT
  [*Aside*] Thus throw I off mine own essential horror,
  And take the shape of a sweet lovely maid   75
  Whom this fool dotes on. We can meet his folly,
  But from his virtues must be runaways.
  We'll sport with him. But when we reckoning call,
  We know where to receive. Th' witch pays for all.

> DOG *barks*

YOUNG BANKS
  Ay? Is that the watchword? She's come. Well, if ever we be   80
  married, it shall be at Barking Church, in memory of thee.
  Now come behind, kind cur.
      And have I met thee, sweet Kate?
      I will teach thee to walk so late.
  O see, we meet in metre. What? Dost thou trip from me?   85
  Oh that I were upon my hobby-horse, I would mount after
  thee so nimble.

---

68 *Katherine's Dock* A landing place along the Thames near St Katherine's
   Hospital, east of the Tower of London; but Young Banks is also fixated here on
   his love for Katherine
73 s.d. *vizarded* masked
75 *shape* Spirits were believed to appear as living or dead persons having no shape
   of their own; here as later with the Spirit of Susan (IV.ii.s.d.69) the boy playing
   Katherine doubled as the Spirit
80 *She's come* Young Banks' simplicity, by which he loves everyone including
   Mother Sawyer, now proves his weakness. He thinks he sees Katherine; later, he
   will spontaneously love Dog (117–18). A central theme of the play is the danger
   of indiscriminate love as well as (with Sir Arthur and Mother Sawyer) indiscriminate dislike
81 *Barking Church* (1) Allhallows, Barking, a church in east London at the east end
   of Great Tower Street; (2) a pun on 'bark'. Punning is also characteristic in
   Rowley's madhouse scenes in *The Changeling*
85 *metre* (1) a reference to lovers, whose language is poetry; (2) a self-referring pun
   on the previous (and subsequent) lines

'Stay nymph, stay, nymph', singed Apollo.
Tarry and kiss me; sweet nymph, stay.
Tarry and kiss me, sweet.   90
We will to Chessum Street,
And then to the house stands in the highway.
Nay, by your leave, I must embrace you.

Ex[*eunt*] SPIR[IT] *and* [YOUNG] BANKS

[*Off stage*] O, help, help, I am drowned, I am drowned.

Enter [YOUNG BANKS] *wet*

DOG
Ha, ha, ha, ha!   95
YOUNG BANKS
This was an ill night to go a-wooing in; I find it now in
Pond's almanac. Thinking to land at Katherine's Dock, I
was almost at Gravesend. I'll never go to a wench in the
dog-days again. Yet 'tis cool enough. Had you never a paw
in this dog-trick? A mangie take that black hide of yours.   100
I'll throw you in at Limehouse in some tanner's pit or other.

88–90 *Stay ... sweet* The chorus of a ballad then popular entitled 'When Daphne
    Did from Phoebus Fly':
    When Daphne from fair Phoebus did fly,
    The west wind most sweetly did blow in her face:
    Her silken scarf scarce shadowed her eyes;
    The god cried 'O pitie', and held her in chase.
    'Stay, nymph, stay nymph,' cries Apollo,
    'Tarry and turn thee; sweet nymph stay!'
88–92 (prose Q)
94 *drowned* Wiggin claims it is characteristic of Rowley to introduce 'whimsical
    burlesque which only too often degenerates into buffoonery and horseplay' (p.
    19); this may be the climax of an extended farcical line which is the core of the
    Young Banks plot
97 *Pond's almanac* (1) An almanac entitled *Enchiridion, or Edward Pond his
    Eutheca*, popular at the time and published each year beginning in 1604 (Pond
    died in 1629); (2) a pun on 'pond'
98 *Gravesend* (1) A port on the south bank of the Thames then 30 miles below
    London; (2) a pun on 'grave'
99 *dog-days* The hottest summer days, from early July to mid-August; dogs were
    thought to go mad at this time (another textual anticipation of later action; cf.
    Anne Ratcliffe, s.d. IV.i.182)
100 *dog-trick* spiteful practical joke
    mangie mange, a disease of a dog's skin
101 *Limehouse* An area then east of London opposite Cuckold's Haven known for
    its tanneries

DOG
Ha, ha, ha, ha.

YOUNG BANKS
How now? Who's that laughs at me? Hist to him. [DOG
barks.] Peace, peace; thou didst but thy kind neither. 'Twas
my own fault.   105

DOG
Take heed how thou trustest the Devil another time.

YOUNG BANKS
How now? Who's that speaks? I hope you have not your
reading tongue about you.

DOG
Yes, I can speak.

YOUNG BANKS
The Devil you can. You have read Aesop's fables then. I   110
have played one of your parts then: the dog that catched at
the shadow in the water. Pray you, let me catechise you a
little. What might one call your name, Dog?

DOG
My dame calls me Tom.

YOUNG BANKS
'Tis well; and she may call me Ass. So there's an whole one   115
betwixt us, Tom-Ass. She said I should follow you, indeed.
Well, Tom, give me thy fist; we are friends. You shall be
mine ingle. I love you, but I pray you let's have no more of
these ducking devices.

DOG
Not, if you love me. Dogs love   120
Where they are beloved. Cherish me,
And I'll do anything for thee.

103 *Hist* listen
104 *but ... neither* what comes naturally to you
108 *reading tongue* preaching tongue
110 *Aesop's fables* Moral tales where animals behave like people
111 *then* (there Q)
111–12 *dog ... water* One of Aesop's tales, in which a dog drops the bone it is carry-
    ing in order to fight its reflection which also carries a bone
112 *catechise* systematically enquire
114 *My ... Tom* From Goodcole: '*Quest. By what name did you call the Diuell, and
    what promises did he make to you? Answ. I did call the Diuell by the name of
    Tom, and he promised to doe for me whatsoeuer I should require of him*' (sig.
    C4)
115 *Ass* foolish (like the animal)
116 *Tom-Ass* Playing on Thomas, the name of Dog never used in the play
118 *ingle* close companion (with homosexual overtones)

YOUNG BANKS

Well you shall have jowls and livers. I have butchers to my
friends that shall bestow 'em. And I will keep crusts and
bones for you, if you'll be a kind dog, Tom.   125

DOG

Anything. I'll help thee to thy love.

YOUNG BANKS

Wilt thou? That promise shall cost me a brown loaf, though
I steal if out of my father's cupboard. You'll eat stolen
goods, Tom, will you not?

DOG

Oh best of all. The sweetest bits, those.   130

YOUNG BANKS

You shall not starve, Ningle Tom; believe that, if you love
fish, I'll help you to maids and soles. I'm acquainted with a
fishmonger.

DOG

Maids and soles? Oh, sweet bits!
Banqueting stuff, those.   135

YOUNG BANKS

One thing I would request you. Ningle, as you have played
the knavish cur with me a little, that you would mingle
amongst our morris-dancers in the morning. You can
dance?

DOG

Yes, yes, anything, I'll be there,   140
But unseen to any but thyself.
Get thee gone before. Fear not my presence.
I have work tonight. I serve more masters,

---

123 *jowls* fish heads (cf. soles, line 132)
    to among
131 *Ningle* ingle (line 118)
131-2 *if ... soles* Young Banks innocently offers food to his new companion, but
    Dog may be attracted by the prurient double meanings by which 'fish' could
    mean 'prostitute', 'maid' a flat fish or harlot and 'soles' souls for the taking. Cf.
    Rowley in *A New Wonder, A Woman Never Vext* (1632):
    Wid[ow]. What fish is there Sirra?
    Clo[wn]. Marry there is Sammon, Pike, and fresh Cod,
              Soles, Maides, and Playce.
    Wid.   Bid, 'm haste to dress 'm them.
    Clo.   Nay mistris, I'le helpe 'm too; the maides shall first
              Dresse the Pike, and the Cod, and then I'le dresse
              The maides in the place you wot on (sig. B2v)
142 *Get ... before* go on ahead
143-4 *I ... one* Cf. 'No servant can serve two masters' (Luke 16:13)

More dames than one.

YOUNG BANKS

[*Aside*] He can serve Mammon and the Devil too.   145

DOG

It shall concern thee, and thy love's purchase.
There's a gallant rival loves the maid;
And likely is to have her. Mark what a mischief
Before the morris ends, shall light on him.

YOUNG BANKS

Oh sweet Ningle, thy neuf once again. Friends must part for   150
a time. Farewell, with this remembrance; shalt have bread
too when we meet again. If ever there were an honest Devil,
'twill be the Devil of Edmonton, I see. Farewell Tom. I
prithee dog me as soon as thou canst.

Ex[*it*] [YOUNG] BANKS

DOG

I'll not miss thee, and be merry with thee.   155
Those that are joys denied must take delight
In sins and mischiefs, 'tis the Devil's right.   *Ex*[*it*] DOG

Act III, Scene ii

Enter YOUNG [FRANK] THORNEY, WINIFRED *as a boy,*
[*crying*]

FRANK

Prithee no more. Those tears give nourishment
To weeds and briars in me, which shortly will
O'ergrow and top my head. My shame will sit

---

145 *Mammon* The god of riches; cf. 'Ye cannot serve God and Mammon' (Matthew
   6:24); also proverbial (M322)
150 *neuf* fist; cf. *A Midsummer Night's Dream*, IV.i.19
153 *Devil of Edmonton* A reference to Peter Fabell, the devil in the other Edmonton
   play, *The Merry Devil of Edmonton* (1607), a source for this play (see
   Introduction). Fabell performs harmless tricks to bring about a marriage that
   faces parental opposition
154 *dog* follow

  0 s.d. 1 (no scene break Q). Winifred's disguise as a boy page is a common theatrical convention; cf. Viola in *Twelfth Night* or Ganymede in *As You Like It*.
   Dekker commonly uses disguises in his plays
  1 *FRANK* Speech prefix in Q reads 'Frank', but in all other cases here 'Y[oung]
   Thor[ney]'

And cover all that can be seen of me.

WINIFRED

I have not shown this cheek in company,   5
Pardon me now. Thus singled with yourself,
It calls a thousand sorrows round about.
Some going before and some on either side;
But infinite behind, all chained together.
Your second adulterous marriage leads;   10
That's the sad eclipse, the effects must follow,
As plagues of shame, spite, scorn and obloquy.

FRANK

Why? Hast thou not left one hour's patience
To add to all the rest? One hour bears us
Beyond the reach of all these enemies.   15
Are we not now set forward in the flight,
Provided with the dowry of my sin,
To keep us in some other nation?
While we together are, we are at home
In any place.

WINIFRED   'Tis foul ill-gotten coin,   20
Far worse than usury or extortion.

FRANK

Let my father then make the restitution,
Who forced me take the bribe. It is his gift
And patrimony to me; so I receive it.
He would not bless, nor look a father on me,   25
Until I satisfied his angry will.
When I was sold, I sold myself again
(Some knaves have done't in lands, and I in body)

5 *cheek* That is, her cheek is covered with tears

6 *singled* alone

7 *It* the cheek

10 *adulterous marriage* While Winifred weeps for Frank's situation she may also be thinking of her own illicit relationship with Sir Arthur

11 *sad eclipse* Often seen as an omen of misfortune; cf. *King Lear*, I.ii.100ff.

14–15 *One ... reach A Match at Midnight* (1607? published 1633), ascribed to Rowley alone, reverses this situation almost exactly: Bloodhound wishes to marry his daughter Moll to a rich informer, but she falls in love with a penniless man whom her father cheated out of his land and runs away with him at midnight, taking with her the deeds to the stolen property. Wiggin claims that some lines are taken from Middleton's plays; Rowley also collaborated with Middleton (Wiggin, pp. 10–11)

27–9 *When ... hire* Frank sees himself as a male prostitute, with his own father as the pander (cf. 95 below)

For money, and I have the hire. But, sweet, no more,
'Tis hazard of discovery, our discourse;   30
And then prevention takes off all our hopes.
For only but to take her leave of me,
My wife is coming.
WINIFRED   Who coming? Your wife?
FRANK
No, no, thou art here. The woman, I knew
Not how to call her now: but after this day   35
She shall be quite forgot, and have no name
In my remembrance. See, see, she's come.

Enter SUSAN

                                        Go lead
The horses to the hill's top, there I'll meet thee.
SUSAN
Nay, with your favour, let him stay a little.
I would part with him too, because he is   40
Your sole companion; and I'll begin with him,
Reserving you the last.
FRANK   Ay, with all my heart.
SUSAN
You may hear, if it please you, sir.
FRANK   No, 'tis not fit.
Some rudiments, I conceive, they must be,
To overlook my slippery footings. And so –   45
SUSAN
No, indeed, sir.
FRANK   Tush, I know it must be so,
And 'tis necessary. On, but be brief.   [*Walks off a little*]
WINIFRED
What charge so'er you lay upon me, mistress,
I shall support it faithfully (being honest)
To my best strength.   50
SUSAN
Believe't shall be no other. I know you were
Commended to my husband by a noble knight.
WINIFRED
Oh gods! Oh, mine eyes!
SUSAN   How now? What ail'st thou, lad?

---

29 *hire* wages, payment
33 *wife* (1) a slip of the tongue; (2) an act of conscience (cf. II.ii.125)
40 *part with* say farewell to
44 *rudiments* basic instructions
45 *so –* (so. Q)
46 *Tush* A common expression of impatience

WINIFRED
  Something hit mine eye, it makes it water still,
  Even as you said 'commended to my husband'.   55
  Some dor I think it was. I was, forsooth,
  Commended to him by Sir Arthur Clarington.
SUSAN
  Whose servant once my Thorney was himself.
  The title methinks should make you almost fellows,
  Or at the least much more than a servant;   60
  And I am sure he will respect you so.
  Your love to him then needs no spur from me,
  And what for my sake you will ever do,
  'Tis fit it should be bought with something more
  Than fair entreats. Look! Here's a jewel for thee,   65
  A pretty wanton label for thine ear;
  And I would have it hang there, still to whisper
  These words to thee, 'Thou hast my jewel with thee'.
  It is but earnest of a larger bounty,
  When thou returnest, with praises of thy service,   70
  Which I am confident thou wilt deserve.
  Why, thou art many now, besides thyself.
  Thou mayst be servant, friend, and wife to him.
  A good wife is them all. A friend can play
  The wife and servant's part, and shift enough.   75
  No less the servant can the friend and wife.
  'Tis all but sweet society, good counsel,
  Interchanged loves, yes; and counsel-keeping.
FRANK [*Returns*] Not done yet?
SUSAN   Even now, sir.
WINIFRED
  Mistress, believe my vow. Your severe eye   80
  Were it present to command; your bounteous hand,
  Were it then by to buy or bribe my service,

---

56 *dor* flying beetle
66 *label* A token to remind Winifred of her pledge to look after Frank; the gift is
   given with mixed feelings and intentions. Cf. Rowley's *All's Lost by Lust*
   I.ii.69–72
68 *my jewel* my chastity; she gave her invaluable virginity to Frank, as compared to
   the money her father has given his father
69 *earnest* (1) instalment; (2) indication
75 *shift* (1) manage; (2) evade; (3) practise fraudulence
79 *Even* just
80 *Your severe eye* In contrast to Mother Sawyer's tongue (as a means of cursing
   and condemning)

Shall not make me more dear or near unto him,
Than I shall voluntary. I'll be all your charge.
Servant, friend, wife to him.
SUSAN   Wilt thou?   85
Now blessings go with thee for't. Courtesies
Shall meet thee coming home.
WINIFRED   Pray you say plainly,
Mistress. Are you jealous of him? If you be,
I'll look to him that way too.
SUSAN   Sayest thou so?
I would thou hadst a woman's bosom now.   90
We have weak thoughts within us. Alas,
There's nothing so strong in us as suspicion.
But I dare not, nay, I will not think
So hardly of my Thorney.
WINIFRED   Believe it, mistress,
I'll be no pander to him; and if I find   95
Any loose lubric scapes in him, I'll watch him,
And at my return, protest I'll show you all.
He shall hardly offend without my knowledge.
SUSAN
Thine own diligence is that I press,
And not the curious eye over his faults.   100
Farewell. If I should never see thee more,
Take it forever.

            [FRANK] *gives his sword*

FRANK
Prithee take that along with thee,
And haste thee to the hill's top;
I'll be there instantly.   *Ex[it]* WIN[IFRED]   105
SUSAN
No haste I prithee, slowly as thou canst.
Pray let him obey me now. 'Tis happily
His last service to me. My power is e'en
A-going out of sight.
FRANK   Why would you delay?
We have no other business now but to part.   110

---

84 *be all your charge* obey your every command
89 *look to* keep watch of
95 *pander* Cf. 27–9 above
96 *lubric scapes* lusty acts of unfaithfulness
102 *it* That is, the label or token
107 *happily* perhaps (by happenstance)

SUSAN

    And will not that, sweetheart, ask a long time?
    Methinks it is the hardest piece of work
    That e'er I took in hand.

FRANK   Fie, fie, why look,
    I'll make it plain and easy to you. Farewell.

Kisses [her]

SUSAN

    Ah, 'las! I am not half perfect in it yet.   115
    I must have it read over an hundred times.
    Pray you take some pains, I confess my dullness.

FRANK

    [*Aside*] What a thorn this rose grows on! Parting were
      sweet,
    But what a trouble 'twill be to obtain it!
    [*To her*] Come, again and again, farewell.

Kisses [her]

                      Yet wilt return?   120
    All questions of my journey, my stay, employment,
    And revisitation, fully I have answered all.
    There's nothing now behind, but nothing.

SUSAN

    And that nothing is more hard than anything,
    Than all the everythings. This request –

FRANK   What is it?   125

SUSAN

    That I may bring you through one pasture more
    Up to yon knot of trees. Amongst those shadows
    I'll vanish from you, they shall teach me how.

FRANK

    Why, 'tis granted. Come, walk then.

SUSAN   Nay, not too fast.
    They say slow things have best perfection.   130
    The gentle shower wets to fertility.

111 *ask* take
117 *take some pains* be patient (with me)
118–19 (Q makes both statements questions)
123 *behind* hidden
127 *yon* yonder
130–4 *They … long* Susan's nervous retreat to proverbial lore resembles her father's
    speech

The churlish storm may mischief with his bounty.
The baser beasts take strength, even from the womb.
But the lord lion's whelp is feeble long.   *Exeunt*

Act III, Scene iii

Enter DOG

DOG
Now for an early mischief and a sudden.
The mind's about it now. One touch from me
Soon sets the body forward.

Enter YOUNG [FRANK] THORNEY, SUSAN

FRANK
Your request is out. Yet will you leave me?
SUSAN
What? So churlishly? You'll make me stay for ever,   5
Rather than part with such a sound from you.
FRANK
Why you almost anger me. Pray you be gone.
You have no company, and 'tis very early;
Some hurt may betide you homewards.
SUSAN   Tush, I fear none.
To leave you is the greatest hurt I can suffer.   10
Besides, I expect your father and mine own,
To meet me back, or overtake me with you.
They began to stir when I came after you.

---

132 *mischief* do damage
134 *lord lion's whelp* Both Pliny in his *Natural History*, VIII.16 (translated by
   Philemon Holland [1601], p. 201), and Topsell, *The Historie of Foure-Footed
   Beastes* (1607), p. 466, comment on the weakness of young lions

  0 s.d. (no new scene in Q)
   Enter DOG Dog, always visible to the audience, is invisible to all the characters
   except Mother Sawyer and Young Banks (and so limited to the underplot); he is
   invisible to characters in the overplot
  1–3 *Now ... forward* Dog's speech suggests he bears final responsibility for the
   death of Susan by bewitching Frank (cf. s.d.14)
  4 *Your ... out* This is as far as you wished to come
   Yet now
  9 *betide* befall
  12 *back* on the way back

I know they'll not be long.
FRANK   [*Aside*] So, I shall have more trouble.

DOG *rubs him*

Thank you for that. Then I'll ease all at once.   15
'Tis done now. What I ne'er thought on.
[*To her*] You shall not go back.
SUSAN   Why?
Shall I go along with thee? Sweet music!
FRANK
No, to a better place.
SUSAN   Any place, I.
I'm there at home, where thou pleasest to have me.   20
FRANK
At home? I'll leave you in your last lodging.
I must kill you.
SUSAN   Oh fine! You'd fright me from you.
FRANK
You see I had no purpose. I'm unarmed.
'Tis this minute's decree, and it must be.
Look, this will serve your turn.

[*Draws his knife*]

SUSAN   I'll not turn from it,   25
If you be earnest, sir. Yet you may tell me
Wherefore you'll kill me.
FRANK   Because you are a whore.
SUSAN
There's one deep wound already. A whore?
'Twas ever further from me than the thought
Of this black hour. A whore?
FRANK   Yes, I'll prove it.   30
And you shall confess it. You are my whore,
No wife of mine. The word admits no second.
I was before wedded to another, have her still.
I do not lay the sin unto your charge,

---

14 s.d. *DOG* The appearance of Dog in Frank's time of need parallels his appearance to Mother Sawyer (II.i.119); it also betrays his inner desires as it does her
  more articulated ones; cf. the next line. 'Of those who ... mentally allied themselves with Satan ... some may have been sinners obsessed by their guilt'
  (Thomas, p. 626)
19 *a better place* heaven
21 *last lodging* coffin
23 *purpose* intention, plan
25 *this* Frank's knife

'Tis all mine own. Your marriage was my theft.   35
For I espoused your dowry, and I have it.
I did not purpose to have added murder;
The Devil did not prompt me. Till this minute
You might have safe returned; now you cannot.
You have dogged your own death.

Stabs her

SUSAN   And I deserve it.   40
I'm glad my fate was so intelligent.
'Twas some good spirit's motion. Die? Oh, 'twas time!
How many years might I have slept in sin?
Sin of my most hatred too, adultery?

FRANK
Nay, sure, 'twas likely that the most was past;   45
For I meant never to return to you
After this parting.
SUSAN   Why then I thank you more,
You have done lovingly, leaving yourself,
That you would thus bestow me on another.
Thou art my husband, Death, and I embrace thee   50
With all the love I have. Forget the stain
Of my unwitting sin. And then I come
A crystal virgin to thee. My soul's purity
Shall with bold wings ascend the doors of Mercy;
For Innocence is ever her companion.   55

FRANK
Not yet mortal? I would not linger you,
Or leave you a tongue to blab.

[Stabs her again]

SUSAN
Now Heaven reward you ne'er the worse for me.
I did not think that death had been so sweet;
Nor I so apt to love him. I could ne'er die better,   60
Had I stayed forty years for preparation.
For I'm in charity with all the world.

---

40 *dogged* persisted in; relentlessly followed to (as in 'dogging my footsteps')
41 *intelligent* clear, understandable
42 *'Twas ... motion* Ironic, since Frank has clearly been at one with Dog; such
      'guardian spirits' were common to witchcraft and Catholic belief but disputed by
      Protestants
45 *the most* the worst
56 *mortal* ready for death   *linger* delay
62 *in charity* at peace

Let me for once be thine example, Heaven;
Do to this man as I him free forgive.
And may he better die, and better live.   65

Moritur [She dies]

FRANK
'Tis done; and I am in. Once past our height,
We scorn the deep'st abyss. This follows now,
To heal her wounds by dressing of the weapon.
Arms, thighs, hands, any place; we must not fail,

Wounds himself

Light scratches giving such deep ones. The best I can   70
To bind myself to this tree. Now's the storm,
Which if blown o'er, many fair days may follow.

DOG *ties him*

So, so, I'm fast; I did not think I could
Have done so well behind me. How prosperous
And effectual mischief sometimes is. Help, help;   75
Murder, murder, murder.

[*Exit* DOG]

Enter [OLD] CARTER *and* OLD THORNEY

OLD CARTER
Ha! Whom tolls the bell for?
FRANK   Oh, oh!
OLD THORNEY   Ah me!

---

65 s.d. *Moritur*. The majority of published accounts in England between 1590 and
   1630 dealing with spousal murder recount the deaths of husbands at the hands
   of their wives. It is likely that the more romantic story of Frank and Susan has
   its roots in the ballad tradition rather than in contemporary history. Lena Cowen
   Orlin notes (p. 252) that 'early domestic tragedy is man-centered, that is, concerned with men's issues. Principal among these issues is the management of
   troublesome women.' This is in inverse parallel to the position of Mother
   Sawyer: nearly all suspected and condemned witches were women, not men
66 *I am in* there is no turning back now
68 *To . . . weapon* to cover up the wounds by putting my blood on the knife
76 s.d. *Exit DOG* (Not in Q; follows RSC production)
77 *tolls the bell* Reference is to the tolling of parish church bells to proclaim a death;
   (1) Old Carter has a premonition in agreement with other anticipations in the
   play; (2) (less likely) Frank's shouts toll like the church bell; (3) (ironically) the
   familiar saying, 'Who does the bell toll for? It tolls for thee' indicating the death
   of his daughter

The cause appears too soon. My child, my son.

OLD CARTER
Susan, girl, child. Not speak to thy father? Ha!

FRANK
O lend me some assistance to o'ertake   80
This hapless woman.

OLD THORNEY   Let's o'ertake the murderers.
Speak whilst thou canst; anon may be too late.
I fear thou hast death's mark upon thee too.

FRANK
I know them both; yet such an oath is passed,
As pulls damnation up if it be broke;   85
I dare not name 'em. Think what forced men do.

OLD THORNEY
Keep oath with murderers? That were a conscience
To hold the Devil in.

FRANK   Nay, sir, I can describe 'em;
Shall show them as familiar as their names.
The taller of the two at this time wears   90
His satin doublet white, but crimson lined;
Hose of black satin, cloak of scarlet.

OLD THORNEY
Warbeck, Warbeck, Warbeck. Do you list to this, sir?

OLD CARTER
Yes, yes, I listen you. Here's nothing to be heard.

FRANK
Th'other's cloak branched velvet, black, velvet-lined   95
His suit.

OLD THORNEY I have 'em already. *Somerton, Somerton.*
Binal revenge, all this. Come, sir, the first work
Is to pursue the murderers, when we have removed
These mangled bodies hence.   100

OLD CARTER
Sir, take that carcass there, and give me this. I'll not own
her now; she's none of mine. Bob me off with a dumb-

---

86 *forced* (1) desperate; (2) play on Frank's own condition of forced marriage and
thus self-referential (cf. II.ii.123ff.)

91 *doublet* tight jacket

94 *Here's ... heard* Old Carter is tragically listening to his dead daughter for signs
of life (cf. *King Lear*, V.iii.264ff.)

95 *branched* embroidered; Frank is proposing a means of identification

98 *Binal* twofold

102 *Bob me off* dismiss me

102–3 *dumb-show* (1) speechless action – here, Susan's body; (2) dumb as silent,
referring to Frank's refusal to name his alleged attackers

show? No, I'll have life. This is my son too, and while
there's life in him, 'tis half mine; take you half that silence   105
for't. When I speak, I look to be spoken to: forgetful slut!

OLD THORNEY
Alas! what grief may do now?
Look, sir, I'll take this load of sorrow with me.

[*Picks up* SUSAN]

OLD CARTER
Ay, do, and I'll have this.

[*Picks up* FRANK]

How do you, sir?
FRANK   O, very ill, sir.
OLD CARTER
Yes, I think so; but 'tis well you can speak yet. There's no
music but in sound, sound it must be. I have not wept these   110
twenty years before, and that I guess was ere that girl was
born. Yet now methinks, if I but knew the way, my heart's
so full, I could weep night and day.

Exeunt

Act III, Scene iv

Enter SIR ARTHUR CLARINGTON, WARBECK, SOMERTON

SIR ARTHUR
Come, gentlemen, we must all help to grace
The nimble-footed youth of Edmonton,
That are so kind to call us up today
With an high morris.

103 *son* son-in-law
107 *load of sorrow* Old Thorney carries Susan

  0 s.d. (no new scene in Q). Although this is a relatively short scene, it is crucial and
     climactic. The morris dance is a spectacle alongside the on-stage murder of Susan
     and must be jolting in its abrupt change of mood. Dog in displacing the Fiddler
     Sawgut restores his first victim (Young Banks) as two other innocent men
     (Warbeck and Somerton) are falsely arrested, ironically bringing both plots
     together
  4 *high* especially merry

WARBECK
  I could wish it for the best, it were   5
  The worst now. Absurdity's in my opinion
  Ever the best dancer in a morris.
SOMERTON
  I could rather sleep than see 'em.
SIR ARTHUR   Not well, sir?
SOMERTON
  Faith not ever thus leaden; yet I know
  No cause for't.
WARBECK   Now am I beyond   10
  Mine own condition highly disposed to mirth.
SIR ARTHUR
  Well, you may have yet a morris to help both;
  To strike you in a dump, and make him merry.

> *Enter* [SAWGUT *the*] *Fiddler and* [*the*] *Morris; all but*
> [YOUNG] BANKS

SAWGUT
  Come, will you set yourselves in morris-ray? The fore-bell,
  second-bell, tenor and great-bell; Maid Marian for the   15
  same bell. But where's the weather-cock now? The hobby-
  horse?
FIRST DANCER
  Is not Banks come yet? What a spite 'tis?
SIR ARTHUR
  When set you forward, gentlemen?
FIRST DANCER
  We stay but for the hobby-horse, sir. All our foot-men are   20
  ready.
SOMERTON
  'Tis marvel your horse should be behind your foot.

---

  9 *not ... leaden* I have never been more depressed
10–11 *beyond ... condition* despite my circumstances
13 *dump* fit of melancholy
14 *SAWGUT* (Fid[d]l[er] Q; also 37–9, 44–7)
   ray array; costumes
16 *weather-cock* The hobby-horse, which shifted like a weather cock because the
   frame is made of light wood
18 *FIRST* (Second Q)
20 *stay* wait
22 *marvel ... foot* In the military, the cavalry preceded the foot-soldiers into battle

SECOND DANCER
Yes, sir. He goes further about. We can come in at the wicket, but the broad gate must be opened for him.

Enter [YOUNG] BANKS, [*as*] *Hobby-horse and* DOG

SIR ARTHUR
O, we stayed for you, sir.   25
YOUNG BANKS
Only my horse wanted a shoe, sir. But we shall make you amends ere we part.
SIR ARTHUR
Ay? Well said, make 'em drink ere they begin.

Enter SERV[ANTS] *with beer*

YOUNG BANKS
A bowl, I prithee, and a little for my horse, he'll mount the better. Nay, give me, I must drink to him, he'll not pledge   30
else. [*Drinks*] Here, hobby.

Holds him the bowl

I pray you. No? Not drink? You see, gentlemen, we can but bring our horse to the water; he may choose whether he'll drink or no.
SOMERTON
A good moral made plain by history.   35
FIRST DANCER
Strike up, Father Sawgut, strike up.
SAWGUT
E'en when you will, children. Now in the name of the best foot forward. How now? Not a word in thy guts? I think, children, my instrument has caught cold on the sudden.
YOUNG BANKS
[*Aside*] My ningle's knavery. Black Tom's doing.   40
ALL
Why, what mean you, Father Sawgut?
YOUNG BANKS
Why what would you have him do? You hear his fiddle is speechless.

---

23 *goes further about* takes the long way around
24 *wicket* small gate
30 *pledge* drink to my health; he offers himself a drink inside the hobby-horse costume
32–4 *we ... no* Proverbial; M262
38 *guts* (1) inner selves; (2) violin strings (made of gut, or animal intestines)

SAWGUT

I'll lay mine ear to my instrument, that my poor fiddle is
bewitched. I played 'The Flowers in May', e'en now, as   45
sweet as a violet; now 'twill not go against the hair. You see
I can make no more music than a beetle of a cow-turd.

YOUNG BANKS

Let me see, Father Sawgut; say, once you had a brave
hobby-horse that you were beholding to. I'll play and dance
too. [Aside] Ningle, away with it.   50

ALL

Ay marry, sir!

> DOG plays the morris; which ended, enter a
> CONSTABLE and OFFICERS

CONSTABLE

Away with jollity, 'tis too sad an hour.
Sir Arthur Clarington, your own assistance,
In the King's name, I charge, for apprehension
Of these two murderers, Warbeck and Somerton.   55

SIR ARTHUR

Ha! Flat murderers?

SOMERTON

Ha, ha, ha, this has awakened my melancholy.

WARBECK

And struck my mirth down flat. Murderers?

CONSTABLE

The accusation is flat against you, gentlemen.
Sir, you may be satisfied with this.   60

> [Shows warrant for their arrest]

I hope you'll quietly obey my power;
'Twill make your cause the fairer.

SOMERTON AND WARBECK [together]

O, with all our hearts, sir.

YOUNG BANKS

[Aside] There's my rival taken up for hangman's meat. Tom
told me he was about a piece of villainy. Mates and morris-   65
men, you see here's no longer piping, no longer dancing.

---

45 'The Flowers ... May' A dance tune no longer extant
46 against the hair 'against the grain' (proverbial)
49 beholding indebted
51 s.d. DOG ... OFFICERS (Q places this before line 51)
54–5 charge ... Somerton Warbeck and Somerton are falsely arrested at Sir
   Arthur's house, while Sir Arthur, guilty of sexual abuse, remains free
62 s.d. SOMERTON AND WARBECK (AMBO [that is, both] Q)

This news of murder has slain the morris. You that go the
foot way, fare ye well. I am for the gallop. Come, Ningle.

Exe[unt YOUNG BANKS *and* DOG]

SAWGUT
[*Strikes his fiddle*] Ay? Nay and my fiddle be come to himself again, I care not. I think the Devil has been abroad   70
amongst us today. I'll keep thee out of thy fit now if I can.

Exe[unt SAWGUT *and* MORRIS DANCERS]

SIR ARTHUR
These things are full of horror, full of pity.
But if this time be constant to the proof,
The guilt of both these gentlemen I dare take
Upon mine own danger; yet howsoever, sir,   75
Your power must be obeyed.
WARBECK   Oh most willingly, sir.
'Tis a most sweet affliction. I could not meet
A joy in the best shape with better will.
Come, fear not, sir; nor judge, nor evidence,
Can bind him o'er, who's freed by conscience.   80
SOMERTON
Mine stands so upright to the middle zone,
It takes no shadow to't, it goes alone.

Exeunt

Act IV, Scene i

Enter OLD BANKS *and two or three* COUNTRYMEN

OLD BANKS
My horse this morning runs most piteously of the glanders,
whose nose yesternight was as clean as any man's here now

---

68 *foot* pedestrian
71 *fit* attack of lunacy
73 *constant* in keeping with
81 *Mine* my conscience
    middle zone equator, denoting balance, perpetual sunlight
82 *goes alone* goes without a shadow

1 *glanders* A contagious disease in horses causing swelling under the jaw and a
   running nose; such an illness often led to accusations of witchcraft

coming from the barber's; and this I'll take my death upon't
is long of this jadish witch, Mother Sawyer.

FIRST COUNTRYMAN

I took my wife and a servingman in our town of Edmonton,   5
thrashing in my barn together, such corn as country
wenches carry to market; and examining my polecat why
she did so, she swore in her conscience she was bewitched.
And what witch have we about us, but Mother Sawyer?

SECOND COUNTRYMAN

Rid the town of her, else all our wives will do nothing else   10
but dance about other country maypoles.

THIRD COUNTRYMAN

Our cattle fall, our wives fall, our daughters fall, and maid-
servants fall; and we ourselves shall not be able to stand, if
this beast be suffered to graze amongst us.

Enter W. HAMLUC, *with thatch and a link*

HAMLUC

Burn the witch, the witch, the witch, the witch.   15

ALL

What hast got there?

---

3 *take* stake

4 *long* on account

5 *took* caught, found

6 *thrashing* (with sexual implications)

7 *polecat* prostitute

11 *maypoles* Brightly coloured poles, decorated with flowers, around which villagers danced on May Day; the poles were regarded as symbols of fertility

12–14 *Our ... us* Such events were the most frequent charges for witchcraft; the
lines also carry sexual implications

14 s.d. *thatch* straw or dry grass. Goodcole writes in *The Wonderfull Discouerie*: 'A
Great, and long suspition was held of this person to be a witch, and the eye of
Mr. *Arthur Robinson*, a worthy Iustice of Peace, who dweleth at *Totnam* neere
to her, was watchfull ouer her, and her wayes, and that not without iust cause;
still hauing his former long suspition of her, by the information of her neighbours that dwelt about her: from suspition, to proceed to great presumptions,
seeing the death of Nurse-children and Cattell, strangely and suddenly to
happen. And to finde out who should bee the author of this mischiefe, an old
ridiculous custome was vsed, which was to plucke the Thatch of her house, and
to burne it, and it being so burned, the author of such mischiefe should presently
then come: and it was obserued and confirmed to the Court, that *Elizabeth
Sawyer* would presently frequent the house of them that burnt the thatch which
they pluckt of her house, and come without any sending for' (sigs. A4–A4v). In
Stuart England, arson was considered a felony

link torch

HAMLUC
A handful of thatch plucked off a hovel of hers. And they
say, when 'tis burning, if she be a witch, she'll come running in.

OLD BANKS
Fire it, fire it. I'll stand between thee and home for any   20
danger.

As that burns, enter the WITCH [SAWYER]

SAWYER
Diseases, plagues; the curse of an old woman
Follow and fall upon you.

ALL
Are you come, you old trot?

OLD BANKS
You hot whore, must we fetch you with fire in your tail?   25

FIRST COUNTRYMAN
This thatch is as good as a jury to prove she is a witch.

ALL
Out, witch; beat her, kick her, set fire on her.

SAWYER
Shall I be murdered by a bed of serpents? Help, help!

Enter SIR ARTHUR CLARINGTON, *and a* JUSTICE

ALL
Hang her, beat her, kill her.

JUSTICE
How now? Forbear this violence.   30

SAWYER
A crew of villains, a knot of bloody hangmen
Set to torment me I know not why.

---

17 *hovel of hers* Mother Sawyer is defending her home; like dunking in which the
accused either drowned or, if not, was condemned, this test of witchcraft cannot
fail to produce as a witch someone already considered guilty

18–19 *burning ... running* a common means both to reveal the guilty and counter
her spells simultaneously

22–3 *curse ... you* a cursing tongue was taken as a certain sign of witchcraft

24 *trot* hag, old woman

25 *hot* lusty

28 s.d. *JUSTICE* The local justice of the peace was the King's representative for all
judicial matters; he used common law which was an imprecise combination of
precedent, custom and statute (see Introduction for the statute pertaining to
witchcraft). The term of service was indefinite, lasting perhaps ten years,
although some JPs in Essex held office for as long as 30 years. Goodcole identifies this one as Arthur Robinson

JUSTICE

Alas, neighbour Banks, are you a ringleader
In mischief? Fie, to abuse an aged woman!

OLD BANKS

Woman? a she-hellcat, a witch. To prove her one, we no   35
sooner set fire on the thatch of her house, but in she came
running, as if the Devil had sent her in a barrel of gun-
powder; which trick as surely proves her a witch, as the pox
in a snuffling nose is a sign a man is a whore-master.

JUSTICE

Come, come; firing her thatch? Ridiculous: 40
Take heed sirs what you do.
Unless your proofs come better armed,
Instead of turning her into a witch,
You'll prove yourselves stark fools.

ALL

Fools?   45

JUSTICE

Arrant fools.

OLD BANKS

Pray, Master Justice What-do-you-call-'um, hear me but in
one thing. This grumbling Devil owes me I know no good
will ever since I fell out with her.

SAWYER

And breakest my back with beating me.   50

OLD BANKS

I'll break it worse.

SAWYER

Wilt thou?

---

39 *snuffling nose* discharge from the nose was believed to indicate syphilis and
reveal that a man was a frequenter of prostitutes

40 *firing her thatch* So Goodcole: 'This triall, though it was slight and ridiculous,
yet it setled a resolution in those whom it concerned, to finde out by all meanes
they could endeauour, her long, and close carried Witchery, to explaine it to the
world; and being descried, to pay in the ende such a worker of Iniquity, her
wages, and that which shee had deserued, (namely, *shame* and *Death*) from
which the Diuell, that had so long deluded her, did not come as shee said, to
shew the least helpe of his vnto her to deliuer her: but being descried in his waies,
and workes, immediately he fled, leauing her to shift and answere for her selfe'
(sig. A4v)

Ridiculous The Justice's forthright exposure of such charges, ensuring sympathy
for Mother Sawyer, contradicts historical fact and is highly unrepresentative of
justices' opinions at the time. Such sympathy is characteristic of Dekker's
thought and playwriting

JUSTICE

You must not threaten her. 'Tis against the law.

[*To* OLD BANKS]

Go on.

OLD BANKS

So, sir, ever since, having a dun cow tied up in my backside,   55
let me go thither, or but cast mine eye at her, and if I should
be hanged, I cannot choose, though it be ten times in an
hour, but run to the cow, and taking up her tail kiss (saving
your worship's reverence) my cow behind; that the whole
town of Edmonton has been ready to bepiss themselves   60
with laughing me to scorn.

JUSTICE

And this is long of her?

OLD BANKS

Who the devil else? For is any man such an ass, to be such
a baby, if he were not bewitched?

SIR ARTHUR

Nay, if she be a witch, and the harms she does   65
End in such sports, she may 'scape burning.

JUSTICE

Go, go; pray vex her not. She is a subject,
And you must not be judges of the law
To strike her as you please.

ALL

No, no, we'll find cudgel enough to strike her.   70

OLD BANKS

Ay, no lips to kiss but my cow's —?

Exeunt [OLD BANKS *and* COUNTRYMEN]

55   *dun* brown
     backside back yard
55–69 *So . . . please* George Gifford records in *A Dialogue Concerning Witches and
     Witchcraftes* (1593), 'A third man came in, and he sayd she [a witch] was once
     angry with him, he had a dun cow which was tyed up in a house, for it was
     winter, he feared that some euill would follow, and for his life he could not come
     in where she was, but he must needes take up her tayle and kisse under it' (sig.
     I4v). The Revels editor notes, 'It is likely that Gifford is the source of Banks'
     anecdote. Certainly Sir Arthur's response and the Justice's admonishment reflect
     something of Gifford's sceptical attitude to witch belief' (p. 241)
58   *saving* apologising in advance because of
60   *bepiss* urinate on
63   *Who . . . else?* A common expression of impatience
66   *burning* In England, accused witches were hanged rather than burned at the
     stake as on the Continent
67   *subject* As a subject of the king, Mother Sawyer holds certain legal rights

SAWYER
  Rots and foul maladies eat up thee and thine.
JUSTICE
  Here's none now, Mother Sawyer,
  But this gentleman, myself, and you;
  Let us to some mild questions; have you mild answers?   75
  Tell us honestly, and with a free confession,
  (We'll do our best to wean you from it)
  Are you a witch, or no?
SAWYER   [*Angrily*] I am none.
JUSTICE
  Be not so furious.
SAWYER
  [*Somewhat calmer*] I am none. None but base curs   80
  So bark at me. I am none.
  Or would I were. If every poor old woman
  Be trod on thus by slaves, reviled, kicked, beaten,
  As I am daily, she, to be revenged,
  Had need turn witch.   85
SIR ARTHUR
  And you to be revenged have sold your soul to th' Devil.
SAWYER
  Keep thine own from him.
JUSTICE
  You are too saucy, and too bitter.
SAWYER
  Saucy? By what commission can he
  Send my soul on the Devil's errand,   90
  More than I can his? Is he
  A landlord of my soul, to thrust it
  When he list out of door?
JUSTICE
  Know whom you speak to.
SAWYER
  A man. Perhaps, no man. Men in gay clothes,   95
  Whose backs are laden with titles and honours,
  Are within far more crooked than I am;
  And if I be a witch, more witch-like.
SIR ARTHUR
  You're a base hell-hound. And now, sir,

76 *free* without duress
80 *curs* scoundrels
93 *list* choose

Let me tell you, far and near she's bruited   100
For a woman that maintains a spirit
That sucks her.
SAWYER   I defy thee.
SIR ARTHUR
Go, go. I can, if need be, bring
An hundred voices, e'en here in Edmonton,
That shall loud proclaim thee for a secret   105
And pernicious witch.
SAWYER   Ha, ha!
JUSTICE
Do you laugh? Why laugh you?
SAWYER
At my name. The brave name this knight gives me – witch!
JUSTICE
Is the name of witch so pleasing to thine ear?
SIR ARTHUR
Pray, sir, give way, and let her tongue gallop on.   110
SAWYER
A witch? Who is not?
Hold not that universal name in scorn then.
What are your painted things in princes' courts?
Upon whose eyelids lust sits blowing fires
To burn men's souls in sensual hot desires.   115
Upon whose naked paps a lecher's thought

---

100 *bruited* rumoured, reported
101–2 *a spirit ... her* Thus Goodcole's account: '*Question. In what places of your
      body did the Diuell sucke of your bloud, and whether did hee himselfe chuse the
      place, or did you your selfe appoint him the place? tell the truth, I charge you,
      as you will answere vnto the Almighty God, and tell the reason if that you can,
      why he would sucke your bloud. Answer.* The place where the Diuell suckt my
      bloud was a little aboue my fundiment, and that place chosen by himselfe; and
      in that place by continuall drawing, there is a thing in the forme of a Teate, at
      which the diuell would suck mee. And I asked the Diuell why hee would sucke
      my bloud, and hee sayd it was to nourish him. *Question. Whether did you pull
      vp your coates or no when the Deuill came to sucke you? Answer.* No I did not,
      but the Diuell would put his head vnder my coates, and I did willingly suffer him
      to doe what hee would. *Question. How long would the time bee, that the Diuell
      would continue sucking of you, and whether did you endure any paine, the time
      that hee was sucking of you? Answer.* He would be sucking of me the continu-
      ance of a quarter of an howre, and when hee suckt me, I then felt no paine at all'
      (sigs. C3–C3v). Cf. s.d.II.i.145
112–15 *Hold ... desires* The playwrights utilize individual psychology here for more
      general satire common to (and of) the period
113 *painted things* women wearing cosmetics

Acts sin in fouler shapes than can be wrought.

JUSTICE
But those work not as you do.

SAWYER   No, but far worse.
These by enchantments can whole lordships change
To trunks of rich attire, turn ploughs and teams   120
To Flanders mares and coaches; and huge trains
Of servitors, to a French butterfly.
Have you not city-witches who can turn
Their husbands' wares, whole standing shops of wares,
To sumptuous tables, gardens of stol'n sin?   125
In one year wasting, what scarce twenty win,
Are not these witches?

JUSTICE   Yes, yes, but the law
Casts not an eye on these.

SAWYER   Why then on me,
Or any lean old beldam? Reverence once
Had wont to wait on age. Now an old woman   130
Ill-favoured grown with years, if she be poor,
Must be called bawd or witch. Such so abused
Are the coarse witches. T'other are the fine,
Spun for the Devil's own wearing.

SIR ARTHUR   And so is thine.

SAWYER
She on whose tongue a whirlwind sits to blow   135
A man out of himself, from his soft pillow,
To lean his head on rocks and fighting waves,
Is not that scold a witch? The man of law
Whose honeyed hopes the credulous client draws,
(As bees by tinkling basins) to swarm to him,   140
From his own hive to work the wax in his;
He is no witch, not he.

---

119 *lordships* estates
121 *Flanders mares* a breed of heavy strong horses bred to draw carriages
122 *servitors* male servants
      French butterfly gaudily dressed, irresponsible person
125 *gardens* Traditionally places of sexual assignation
130 *wont* accustomed
130-2 *Now ... witch* This definition closely follows that of Reginald Scot (see note
      to II.i.3–4); that the playwrights make use of Scot and Gifford suggests their own
      scepticism concerning witchcraft beliefs and procedures
132 *bawd* procuress
140-1 *bees ... his* According to popular belief, bees could be summoned by banging
      on pots and pans; Thomas Tusser in *Five Hundred Points of Good Husbandry*
      says this was a way to claim ownership of them

SIR ARTHUR   But these men-witches
  Are not in trading with hell's merchandise,
  Like such as you are, that for a word, a look,
  Denial of a coal of fire, kill men,   145
  Children and cattle.
SAWYER   Tell them, sir, that do so.
  Am I accused for such an one?
SIR ARTHUR   Yes, 'twill be sworn.
SAWYER
  Dare any swear I ever tempted maiden
  With golden hooks flung at her chastity,
  To come and lose her honour? And being lost,   150
  To pay not a denier for't? Some slaves have done it.
  Men-witches can without the fangs of law,
  Drawing once one drop of blood, put counterfeit pieces
  Away for true gold.
SIR ARTHUR   By one thing she speaks,
  I know now she's a witch, and dare no longer   155
  Hold conference with the fury.
JUSTICE   Let's then away.
  Old woman, mend thy life, get home and pray.

                Exeunt [SIR ARTHUR CLARINGTON *and* JUSTICE]

SAWYER
  For his confusion.

                        Enter DOG

                    My dear Tom-boy welcome.
  I am torn in pieces by a pack of curs
  Clapped all upon me, and for want of thee.   160
  Comfort me. Thou shalt have the teat anon.
DOG
  Bow, wow. I'll have it now.
SAWYER   I am dried up
  With cursing and with madness; and have yet

---

151 *denier* A French copper coin of little value
154–6 *By ... fury* Another anticipation as well as a motive for attacking Mother
     Sawyer: Sir Arthur thinks that using the witch's power to divine relationships,
     Mother Sawyer has recognised his affair with Winifred
158 *dear Tom-boy* Mother Sawyer's ready acceptance of Dog betrays the friendly
     Justice's departing caution suggesting the power of a village's condemnation of
     a woman like her
160 *Clapped* set upon forcefully
162–3 *dried ... cursing* Mother Sawyer claims a choleric temperament, both a physi-
     cal and medical condition

No blood to moisten these sweet lips of thine.
Stand on thy hind-legs up. Kiss me, my Tommy,   165
And rub away some wrinkles on my brow
By making my old ribs to shrug for joy
Of thy fine tricks. What hast thou done? Let's tickle.

[*They embrace*]

Hast thou struck the horse lame as I bid thee?
DOG
Yes, and nipped the suckling child.
SAWYER   Ho, ho, my dainty,   170
My little pearl. No lady loves her hound,
Monkey, or parakeet, as I do thee.
DOG
The maid has been churning butter nine hours;
But it shall not come.
SAWYER
Let 'em eat cheese and choke.
DOG   I had rare sport   175
Among the clowns i'th'morris.
SAWYER   I could dance
Out of my skin to hear thee. But, my curl-pate,
That jade, that foul-tongued whore, Nan Ratcliffe,

---

167 *shrug* moving the body from side to side as a sign of joy
168 *tickle* become affectionate. Again Mother Sawyer condemns herself. In the 1984
      Bristol production, Mother Sawyer tickled Dog's stomach; in the 1981 RSC pro-
      duction, the two rolled on the floor together
171 *pearl* Then a common name for a dog
173–4 *The ... come* So Reginald Scot in *The Discouerie of Witchcraft* (1584): 'They
      can also bring to passe, that chearne as long as you list, your butter will not
      come; especiallie if either the maids haue eaten vp the creame; or the goodwife
      haue sold the butter before in the market. Whereof I haue had some triall,
      although there may be true and naturall causes to hinder the common course
      thereof: as for example. Put a little sope or sugar into your chearne of creame,
      and there will neuer come anie butter, chearne as long as you list' (1.4; p. 11)
177 *curl-pate* curly-headed person (an affectionate term)
178–81 *That ... heart?* The playwrights return here to recorded history. According
      to Goodcole, 'She was also indited, for that shee the said *Elizabeth Sawyer*, by
      Diabolicall helpe, and out of her malice afore-thought, did witch vnto death
      Agnes Ratcleife, a neighbour of hers, dwelling in the towne of *Edmonton* where
      shee did likewise dwell, and the cause that vrged her thereunto was, because that
      Elizabeth Ratceife [sic] did strike a Sowe of hers in her sight, for licking vp a little
      Soape where shee had laide it, and for that *Elizabeth Sawyer* would be reuenged
      of her' (sigs. B1v–B2)

Who for a little soap licked by my sow,
Struck, and almost had lamed it. Did not I charge thee   180
To pinch that quean to th'heart?

DOG

Bow, wow, wow. Look here else.

Enter ANNE RATCLIFFE *mad*

RATCLIFFE

See, see, see; the Man i'th' Moon has built a new windmill,
and what running there's from all quarters of the city to
learn the art of grinding!   185

SAWYER

Ho, ho, ho! I thank thee, my sweet mongrel.

RATCLIFFE

Hoyda! A pox of the Devil's false hopper! All the golden
meal runs into the rich knaves' purses, and the poor have
nothing but bran. Hey derry down! Are you not Mother
Sawyer?   190

SAWYER

No, I am a lawyer.

RATCLIFFE

Art thou? I prithee let me scratch thy face; for thy pen has
flayed off a great many men's skins. You'll have brave
doings in the vacation; for knaves and fools are at variance
in every village. I'll sue Mother Sawyer, and her own sow   195
shall give in evidence against her.

SAWYER

[*To* DOG] Touch her.

181 *pinch ... th'heart?* kill her
    quean whore
185 *grinding* (1) to grind corn; (2) to pimp or extort (cf. Job 31:10)
187 *Hoyda!* a nonsense exclamation
    hopper a container through which grain passes for grinding
189 *Hey derry down!* A common refrain from songs
192 *scratch thy face* A common way to disempower a witch was to draw her blood
    (or her *malificium*) out of her. 'A good countrey Yeoman', an 'honest man', 'per-
    swaded himselfe, by such a one she was bewitched and hee was as faithfully per-
    swaded, that if he could but have 2 or 3 good scratches, at her face, wherby he
    might draw blood of her, he should recouer presently' (*The seuerall practises of
    Iohane Harnson, and her daughter, condemned and executed at Hartford, for
    Witch craft, the 4 of August last, 1606* [1607], sigs. C3–C3v); cf. George Gifford
    in *A Dialogue Concerning Witches and Witchcraftes* (1593): 'What say you to
    the boy which healed within few daies af[ter] he had scratched the witch,
    whereas his sores were most grieuous before, and could not be cured?' (sig. H1)
194 *vacation* The period when law courts were not in session

[DOG *rubs against* ANNE RATCLIFFE]

RATCLIFFE
Oh my ribs are made of a paned hose, and they break.
There's a Lancashire hornpipe in my throat. Hark how it
tickles it, with doodle, doodle, doodle, doodle. Welcome   200
sergeants: welcome Devil. Hands, hands; hold hands, and
dance around, around, around.

Enter OLD BANKS, *his son* [YOUNG BANKS] *the Clown*,
OLD RATCLIFFE [*and*] COUNTRY-FELLOWS

OLD RATCLIFFE
She's here; alas, my poor wife is here.

OLD BANKS
Catch her fast, and have her into some close chamber. Do,
for she's as many wives are, stark mad.   205

YOUNG BANKS
The witch, Mother Sawyer, the witch, the Devil.

OLD RATCLIFFE
O, my dear wife! Help, sirs!

[OLD RATCLIFFE *and the* COUNTRY-FELLOWS] *car*[*ry*]
her off

OLD BANKS
You see your work, Mother Bumby.

197 *Touch her* Mother Sawyer's vicious command to harm a neighbour with whom
she has a trifling quarrel complicates the reaction to a character who has been
sympathetically portrayed

198–202 *Oh ... around* Anne Ratcliffe's madness draws on Bedlam scenes in
Dekker's *Honest Whore Part I* as well as on contemporary scenes of madness in
Senecan tragedy and the Londoner's experiences seeing Bedlamites

198 *paned hose* breeches of cloth strips of various colours

199 *Lancashire hornpipe* (1) a wind instrument similar to a clarinet; (2) a lively
dance. In 1612 Lancashire underwent 'an epidemic' of witchcraft when 12 persons were executed

200 *doodle ... doodle* A sound imitating a hornpipe

201 *sergeants* court officers
welcome Devil Anne Ratcliffe is bewitched

204 *close* (1) locked; (2) small; (3) confining

208 *Mother Bumby* The title character in John Lyly's comedy (1589) who was, prop-
erly speaking, a wise woman and not a witch – that is, a woman who used her
special powers for healing others. But the term was later applied to women who
used power for evil ends. T. I. mentions in *A World of wonders* (1595) 'I might
heere noate the cruell deuises of mother *Bumby* the witch of *Rochester*: the tiran-
nie of the witches of *Warboys*, and many other' (sig. E4)

SAWYER

My work? Should she and all you here run mad,
Is the work mine?   210

YOUNG BANKS

No, on my conscience, she would not hurt a Devil of two
years old.

Enter OLD RATCLIFFE *and the rest*

How, now? What's become of her?

OLD RATCLIFFE

Nothing. She's become nothing, but the miserable trunk of
a wretched woman. We were in her hands as reeds in a   215
mighty tempest. Spite of our strengths, away she brake; and
nothing in her mouth being heard, but 'the Devil, the witch,
the witch, the Devil'; she beat out her own brains, and so
died.

YOUNG BANKS

It's any man's case, be he never so wise, to die when his   220
brains go a-wool-gathering.

OLD BANKS

Masters, be ruled by me; let's all to a Justice. Hag, thou
hast done this, and thou shalt answer it.

SAWYER

Banks, I defy thee.

OLD BANKS

Get a warrant first to examine her, then ship her to   225
Newgate. Here's enough, if all her other villainies were par-
doned, to burn her for a witch. You have a spirit, they say,
comes to you in the likeness of a dog; we shall see your cur
at one time or other. If we do, unless it be the Devil himself, he shall go howling to the gaol in one chain, and thou   230
in another.

211–12 *she ... old* Cf. 'She would not harm a fly', 'There's no more harm in him than
   in a devil of two years old', both proverbial

218 *beat out her own brains* T. I. in *A World of wonders* (1595) recounts the 'facts'
   of 'a Witch named mother white-coate alias mother *Arnold alias* mother
   Glassenbury' of Barking who drives the fishermen Thomas Clark and William
   Daulbie to attempt suicide (sigs. E2v–E3)

219 *died* Mother Sawyer becomes indirectly responsible for Anne Ratcliffe's death in
   opposition to Frank who is directly responsible for Susan's

221 *brains go a-wool-gathering* Proverbial (W582)

225 *ship* convey

226 *Newgate* A London prison for felons; Elizabeth Sawyer, incarcerated there, thus
   came in contact with Henry Goodcole who was her 'continuall visitor' (see
   Introduction)

230 *gaol* (goal Q)

SAWYER
Be hanged thou in a third, and do thy worst.
YOUNG BANKS
How, Father? You send the poor dumb thing howling to th'
gaol? He that makes him howl, makes me roar.
OLD BANKS
Why, foolish boy, dost thou know him?   235
YOUNG BANKS
No matter, if I do or not. He's bailable I am sure by law.
But if the dog's word will not be taken, mine shall.
OLD BANKS
Thou bail for a dog?
YOUNG BANKS
Yes, or a bitch either, being my friend. I'll lie by the heels
myself, before Puppison shall. His dog-days are not come   240
yet, I hope.
OLD BANKS
What manner of dog is it? Didst ever see him?
YOUNG BANKS
See him? Yes, and given him a bone to gnaw twenty times.
The dog is no court-foisting hound, that fills his belly full
by base wagging his tail; neither is it a citizen's water-   245
spaniel, enticing his master to go a-ducking twice or thrice
a week, whilst his wife makes ducks and drakes at home.
This is no Paris-garden bandog neither, that keeps a bow-
wow-wowing, to have butchers bring their curs thither, and
when all comes to all, they run away like sheep. Neither is   250
this the Black Dog of Newgate.

232 *in a third* quickly
233 *poor dumb thing* That is, Dog, not Mother Sawyer
239 *lie by the heels* (1) put in the stocks; (2) put in chains
240 *Puppison* An affectionate term for puppy
    dog-days days of suffering (and possibly death); see note to III.i.99
244 *court-foisting hound* The common term of contempt for a lapdog
247 *makes ducks and drakes* has illicit affairs; proverbial (D632)
248 *Paris-garden* A bear-baiting arena in Southwark near the theatres
    bandog fierce mastiff used to bait bears or bulls
251 *Black Dog of Newgate* A black dog, commonly believed an evil spirit haunting
    Newgate prison; *The Black Dog of Newgate*, a popular pamphlet by the high-
    wayman Luke Hutton published in 1596, has the dog represent not the Devil but
    the corrupt (devilish) practices of the prison guards such as false arrests and bilk-
    ing victims. In 1598 *Luke Huttons Lamentacion*, one of many ballads on the
    same theme, appeared

OLD BANKS
  No, Goodman Son-fool, but the Dog of Hell-gate.
YOUNG BANKS
  I say, Goodman Father-fool, it's a lie.
ALL
  He's bewitched.
YOUNG BANKS
  A gross lie as big as myself. The Devil in St Dunstan's will 255
  as soon drink with this poor cur, as with any Temple-bar
  laundress that washes and wrings lawyers.

                    [*Enter* DOG]

DOG
  Bow, wow, wow, wow.
ALL
  O the Dog's here, the Dog's here.
OLD BANKS
  It was the voice of a dog.   260
YOUNG BANKS
  The voice of a dog? If that voice were a dog's, what voice
  had my mother? So I am a dog. Bow, wow, wow. It was I
  that barked so, Father, to make coxcombs of these clowns.
OLD BANKS
  However, we'll be coxcombed no longer. Away therefore to
  th' Justice for a warrant; and then, Gammer Gurton, have 265
  at your needle of witchcraft.
SAWYER
  And prick thine own eyes out. Go, peevish fools.

       Exeunt [OLD BANKS, OLD RATCLIFFE *and* COUNTRYMEN]

YOUNG BANKS
  Ningle, you had like to have spoiled all with your bowings.
  I was glad to put 'em off with one of my dog-tricks on a
  sudden; I am bewitched, little cost-me-nought, to love thee 270

252 *Goodman* A common term of address for yeomen and farmers
     Dog of Hell-gate According to the myth, Cerberus
255 *Devil in St Dunstan's* Devil Tavern in Fleet Street near St Dunstan's Church and
     next to Temple Bar, one of the Inns of Court (named for the tavern sign in which
     St Dunstan pulls on the Devil's nose with pincers)
257 *laundress* A cant term for whore
265 *warrant* An order to commit to prison; cf. the false accusations of Warbeck and
     Somerton
     Gammer Gurton A bewitching storyteller who has the title-role in a comedy by
     W. Stevenson (1553); the farce is centred on the search for her lost needle (with
     sexual implications)

– a pox, that morris makes me spit in thy mouth. I dare not
stay. Farewell, Ningle; you whoreson dog's nose. Farewell
witch.   *Exit*

DOG

Bow, wow, wow, wow.

SAWYER

Mind him not, he's not worth thy worrying.   275
Run at a fairer game. That foul-mouthed knight,
Scurvy Sir Arthur, fly at him, my Tommy;
And pluck out's throat.

DOG

No, there's a dog already biting's conscience.

SAWYER

That's a sure bloodhound. Come, let's home and play.   280
Our black work ended, we'll make holiday.

                                                    Exeunt

Act IV, Scene ii

Enter KATHERINE: *a bed thrust forth, on it* FRANK *in a
slumber*

KATHERINE

Brother, brother! So sound asleep? That's well.

FRANK

No, not I, sister. He that's wounded here,
As I am; (all my other hurts are bitings
Of a poor flea) but he that here once bleeds,
Is maimed incurably.

KATHERINE   My good sweet brother,   5
(For now my sister must grow up in you)
Though her loss strikes you through, and that I feel
The blow as deep, I pray thee be not cruel
To kill me too, by seeing you cast away
In your own helpless sorrow. Good love, sit up.   10
And if you can give physic to yourself,

---

271 *spit in thy mouth* want to please you; from the common belief that dogs liked
    people who spat in their mouths
272 *whoreson dog's nose* Here a term of endearment
279 *biting's conscience* Perhaps a further reference to Dog's awareness of Sir Arthur's
    affair with Winifred

3–4 *bitings ... flea* 'It is but a flea-biting' is proverbial (F355), but cf. IV.i.279
11 *physic* medicine, treatment

I shall be well.

FRANK   I'll do my best.

KATHERINE   I thank you.
What do you look about for?

FRANK   Nothing, nothing.
But I was thinking, sister.

KATHERINE   Dear heart, what?

FRANK
Who but a fool would thus be bound to a bed,   15
Having this room to walk in?

KATHERINE   Why do you talk so?
Would you were fast asleep.

FRANK   No, no; I'm not idle.
But here's my meaning. Being robbed as I am,
Why should my soul, which married was to hers,
Live in divorce, and not fly after her?   20
Why should not I walk hand in hand with death
To find my love out?

KATHERINE   That were well, indeed.
Your time being come, when death is sent to call you,
No doubt you shall meet her.

FRANK   Why should not I go
Without calling?

KATHERINE   Yes, brother, so you might,   25
Were there no place to go to when you're gone,
But only this.

FRANK   Troth, sister, thou sayest true.
For when a man has been an hundred years,
Hard travelling o'er the tottering bridge of age,
He's not the thousand part upon his way.   30
All life is but a wandering to find home.
When we are gone, we are there. Happy were man
Could here his voyage end; he should not then
Answer how well or ill he steered his soul,
By heaven's or by hell's compass; how he put in   35
(Losing blessed goodness' shore) at such a sin;
Nor how life's dear provision he has spent.
Nor how far he in's navigation went
Beyond commission. This were a fine reign,
To do ill, and not hear of it again.   40
Yet then were man more wretched than a beast.
For, sister, our dead pay is sure the best.

KATHERINE
'Tis so, the best or worst. And I wish heaven

17 *idle* delirious

To pay (and so I know it will) that traitor,
That devil Somerton (who stood in mine eye   45
Once as an angel) home to his deservings.
What villain but himself, once loving me,
With Warbeck's soul would pawn his own to hell,
To be revenged on my poor sister?
FRANK   Slaves!
A pair of merciless slaves! Speak no more of them.   50
KATHERINE
I think this talking hurts you.
FRANK   Does me no good, I'm sure.
I pay for't everywhere.
KATHERINE   I have done then.
Eat, if you cannot sleep. You have these two days
Not tasted any food. Jane, is it ready?
FRANK
What's ready? What's ready?   55

          [JANE *enters with a plate of chicken*]

KATHERINE
I have made ready a roasted chicken for you.
Sweet, wilt thou eat?
FRANK   A pretty stomach on a sudden – yes –
There's one in the house can play upon a lute.
Good girl, let's hear him too.
KATHERINE   You shall, dear brother.

                              [*Exit* JANE]

Would I were a musician, you should hear   60
How I would feast your ear.

                    Lute plays

                    Stay, mend your pillow,
And raise you higher.
FRANK   I am up too high.
Am I not, sister, now?
KATHERINE   No, no, 'tis well.
Fall to, fall to. A knife. Here's never a knife.
Brother, I'll look out yours. [*She searches his clothes*]

     Enter DOG, *shrugging as it were for joy, and dances*

FRANK   Sister, O sister,   65
I am ill upon a sudden; and can eat nothing.

65 s.d. *joy* Dog is happy at his ability to expose Frank

KATHERINE
In very deed you shall. The want of food
Makes you so faint. [*Finds knife but does not remove it*]
      Ha! Here's none in your pocket.
I'll go fetch a knife.   *Exit*
FRANK   Will you? 'Tis well, all's well.

> *She gone, he searches first one, then the other pocket.*
> *Knife found.* DOG *runs off. He lies on one side. The*
> SPIRIT *of* SUSAN *his second wife comes to the bed-side.*
> *He stares at it, and turning to the other side, it's there*
> *too. In the meantime,* WINIFRED *as a page comes in,*
> *stands at his bed's feet sadly. He frighted, sits upright.*
> *The* SPIRIT *vanishes.*

FRANK
What art thou?
WINIFRED   A lost creature.
FRANK   So am I too.   70
Win? Ah, my she-page!
WINIFRED   For your sake I put on
A shape that's false; yet do I wear a heart
True to you as your own.
FRANK   Would mine and thine
Were fellows in one house. Kneel by me here.
On this side now? How dar'st thou come to mock me   75
On both sides of my bed?
WINIFRED   When?
FRANK   But just now.
Outface me, stare upon me with strange postures.
Turn my soul wild by a face in which were drawn
A thousand ghosts leapt newly from their graves,
To pluck me into a winding-sheet.
WINIFRED   Believe it,   80
I came no nearer to you than yon place,
At your bed's feet; and of the house had leave,

---

68 s.d. [*Finds knife ...*] The discovery of the knife with Susan's blood on it is a
strong but problematic image: did Frank overlook this in his emotional state
during the murder, deliberately hide it and then later forget about it, or keep it
out of a sense of guilt, hoping it might later be discovered?

69 s.d. *SPIRIT of SUSAN* (1) A sign of Frank's sense of guilt projected in a ghost
of his creation; (2) an act of the Devil, perhaps through the agency of Dog.
Susan's ghost has not returned to accuse Frank, in all probability, since she for-
gave him at the time of her death. Goodcole says scurrilous ballads reported
'Spirits' attending Mother Sawyer in prison (sig. A3v)

79 *ghosts ... graves* A common belief held that ghosts announced impending deaths

Calling myself your horse-boy, in to come,
And visit my sick master.
FRANK   Then 'twas my fancy.
Some windmill in my brains for want of sleep.   85
WINIFRED
Would I might never sleep, so you could rest.
But you have plucked a thunder on your head,
Whose noise cannot cease suddenly. Why should you
Dance at the wedding of a second wife?
When scarce the music which you heard at mine   90
Had ta'en a farewell of you. O this was ill!
And they who thus can give both hands away,
In th'end shall want their best limbs.
FRANK   Winifred,
The chamber-door fast?
WINIFRED   Yes.
FRANK   Sit thee then down;
And when thou hast heard me speak, melt into tears.   95
Yet I to save those eyes of thine from weeping,
Being to write a story of us two,
Instead of ink, dipped my sad pen in blood.
When of thee I took leave, I went abroad
Only for pillage, as a freebooter,   100
What gold soe'er I got, to make it thine.
To please a father, I have Heaven displeased.
Striving to cast two wedding rings in one,
Through my bad workmanship I now have none.
I have lost her and thee.
WINIFRED   I know she's dead.   105
But you have me still.
FRANK   Nay, her this hand
Murdered; and so I lose thee too.
WINIFRED   Oh me!
FRANK
Be quiet, for thou my evidence art,
Jury and judge. Sit quiet and I'll tell all.

As they whisper, enter at one end of the stage OLD
CARTER *and* KATHERINE, DOG *at the other, pawing
softly at* FRANK

85 *Some ... sleep* Proverbial (W455). Cf. *The Merry Devil of Edmonton*: 'what, are
   your braines alwayes water-milles? must they euer runne round?' (II.i.3–4)
100 *pillage ... freebooter* Frank is confessing his deeds metaphorically, perhaps
   unable yet to face the truth of his actions directly
   freebooter pirate
109 s.d. *DOG ... FRANK* This action shows Dog maintains his control over Frank

KATHERINE
    I have run madding up and down to find you,   110
    Being laden with the heaviest news that ever
    Poor daughter carried.
OLD CARTER   Why? Is the boy dead?
KATHERINE
    Dead, sir! O, Father, we are cozened. You are told
    The murderer sings in prison, and he laughs here.
    This villain killed my sister. See else, see,   115
    A bloody knife in's pocket.
OLD CARTER   Bless me, patience!
FRANK
    The knife, the knife, the knife!
KATHERINE
    What knife?

                                                    Exit DOG

FRANK   To cut my chicken up, my chicken;
    Be you my carver, Father.
OLD CARTER   That I will.
KATHERINE
    [*Aside*] How the Devil steels our brows after doing ill!   120
FRANK
    My stomach and my sight are taken from me;
    All is not well within me.
OLD CARTER
    I believe thee, boy. I that have seen so many moons clap
    their horns on other men's foreheads to strike them sick, yet
    mine to 'scape and be well! I that never cast away a fee   125
    upon urinals, but am as sound as an honest man's con-
    science when he's dying, I should cry out as thou dost, 'All
    is   not   well   within   me',   felt   I   but   the   bag   of   thy

110 *madding* anxiously
113 *cozened* deceived
114 *The ... prison* Common belief (and tradition) held that a prisoner sang just
    before his death
115 *See else* If you do not believe me
124 *horns* sign of a cuckold; Old Carter tells Frank he knows of his guilt (since
    Katherine told him of the knife at 116)
126 *urinals* When a sick man's health was in doubt, glass vessels of urine were sent
    to a medical examiner. Old Carter has no doubt of Frank's guilt and does not
    wish to waste money on such tests
128 *bag* sack in the body containing poison
129 *impostumes* swellings or cysts; that is, physical (perhaps demonstrating moral)
    corruption

imposthumes. Ah poor villain! Ah my wounded rascal! All
my grief is, I have now small hope of thee.   130

FRANK
Do the surgeons say, my wounds are dangerous then?

OLD CARTER
Yes, yes, and there's no way with thee but one.

FRANK
Would he were to open them.

OLD CARTER
I'll go to fetch him. I'll make an holiday to see thee as I
wish.   *Exit to fetch* OFFICERS   135

FRANK
A wondrous kind old man.

WINIFRED
[*Aside*] Your sin's the blacker, so to abuse his goodness.
[*To* FRANK] Master, how do you?

FRANK   Pretty well now, boy.
I have such odd qualms come 'cross my stomach!
I'll fall to. Boy, cut me.

WINIFRED   [*Aside*] You have cut me, I'm sure.   140
[*To* FRANK] A leg or wing, sir.

FRANK   No, no, no. A wing?
[*Aside*] Would I had wings but to soar up yon tower.
But here's a clog that hinders me.

> [*Enter*] FATHER [OLD CARTER] *with* [SUSAN'S *body*] *in a*
> *coffin* [*carried by* SERVANTS]

                                   What's that?

OLD CARTER
That? What? O, now I see her, 'tis a young wench, my
daughter, sirrah, sick to the death. And hearing thee to be   145
an excellent rascal for letting blood, she looks out at a case-
ment, and cries, 'Help, help', 'stay that man'; 'him I must
have, or none'.

FRANK
For pity's sake, remove her. See, she stares
With one broad open eye still in my face.   150

---

132 *there's ... one* Proverbial (W148)

137 *Your ... goodness* The line is deeply problematic. While Winifred seems to wres-
tle with her conscience over Frank's murder – performed (as he saw it) for her
sake – she may also be recalling that her silence over the affair with Sir Arthur
which led to her marriage makes her complicit in the murder as well

146 *letting blood* According to popular belief, a corpse bled again when confronted
by its killer

150 *one broad open eye* Frank suffers another attack of conscience in Susan's second
unexpected appearance (cf. III.ii.37)

OLD CARTER
  Thou puttest both hers out, like a villain as thou art; yet
  see, she is willing to lend thee one again to find out the mur-
  derer, and that's thyself.

FRANK
  Old man, thou liest.

OLD CARTER
  So shalt thou i'th'gaol. Run for officers.   155

KATHERINE
  O thou merciless slave! She was
  (Though yet above ground) in her grave
  To me, but thou hast torn it up again. Mine eyes
  Too much drowned, now must feel more rain.

OLD CARTER
  Fetch officers.   160

                                        Exit KATHERINE

FRANK
  For whom?

OLD CARTER
  For thee, sirrah, sirrah. Some knives have foolish posies
  upon them, but thine has a villainous one; look. Oh! it is
  enamelled with the heart-blood of thy hated wife, my
  beloved daughter. What sayst thou to this evidence? Is't not   165
  sharp? Does't not strike home? Thou canst not answer honestly, and without a trembling heart, to this one point, this
  terrible bloody point.

WINIFRED
  I beseech you, sir. Strike him no more;
  You see he's dead already.   170

OLD CARTER
  O, sir! You held his horses, you are as arrant a rogue as he.
  Up, go you too.

FRANK
  As you're a man, throw not upon that woman
  Your loads of tyranny, for she's innocent.

OLD CARTER
  How? How? A woman? Is't grown to a fashion for women   175
  in all countries to wear the breeches?

WINIFRED
  I am not as my disguise speaks me, sir, his page;
  But his first only wife, his lawful wife.

155 gaol (goal Q)
162 *posies* mottoes, verses

OLD CARTER
  How? How? More fire i'th'bedstraw?
WINIFRED
  The wrongs which singly fell upon your daughter,   180
  On me are multiplied. She lost a life,
  But I, an husband and myself must lose,
  If you call him to a bar for what he has done.
OLD CARTER
  He has done it then?
WINIFRED
  Yes, 'tis confessed to me.
FRANK   Dost thou betray me?   185
WINIFRED
  O, pardon me, dear heart! I am mad to lose thee,
  And know not what I speak. But if thou didst,
  I must arraign this father for two sins,
  Adultery and murder.

                    Enter KATHERINE

KATHERINE   Sir, they are come.
OLD CARTER
  Arraign me for what thou wilt, all Middlesex knows me   190
  better for an honest man than the middle of a market-place
  knows thee for an honest woman. Rise, sirrah, and don
  your tacklings, rig yourself for the gallows, or I'll carry thee
  thither on my back. Your trull shall to the gaol go with you;
  there be as fine Newgate birds as she that can draw him in. 195
  Pox on's wounds.
FRANK
  I have served thee, and my wages now are paid.
  Yet my worst punishment shall, I hope, be stayed.

                                        Exeunt

179 *fire i'th' bedstraw* more hidden mischief; proverbial (F272)
188 *father* Winifred accuses Frank of her pregnancy (thus concealing her affair with
    Sir Arthur) but Old Carter, confused and culpable, thinks she means him in the
    following lines. Presumably the playwrights use this occasion to show how wide-
    spread complicity and guilt are in socially constructed victims, for Winifred is
    otherwise treated sympathetically
193 *tacklings* clothes
    I'll carry thee A puzzling allusion to the customary image of the Devil carrying
    a sinner off to Hell
194 *trull* strumpet, prostitute
    gaol (goal Q) Dekker himself was in debtors' prison from 1613 to 1619
198 *worst punishment* damnation

Act V, Scene i

Enter MOTHER SAWYER *alone*

SAWYER

Still wronged by every slave? And not a dog
Bark in his dame's defence? I am called witch,
Yet am myself bewitched from doing harm.
Have I given up myself to thy black lust
Thus to be scorned? Not see me in three days?   5
I'm lost without my Tomalin. Prithee come,
Revenge to me is sweeter far than life;
Thou art my raven, on whose coal-black wings
Revenge comes flying to me. O my best love!
I am on fire, (even in the midst of ice)   10
Raking my blood up, till my shrunk knees feel
Thy curled head leaning on them. Come then, my darling.
If in the air thou hover'st, fall upon me
In some dark cloud, and as I oft have seen
Dragons and serpents in the elements,   15
Appear thou now so to me. Art thou i'th'sea?
Muster up all the monsters from the deep,
And be the ugliest of them. So that my bulch
Show but his swart cheek to me, let earth cleave,
And break from hell, I care not. Could I run   20
Like a swift powder-mine beneath the world,
Up would I blow it all, to find out thee,
Though I lay ruined in it. Not yet come!
I must then fall to my old prayer.
Sanctibiceter nomen tuum.   25
Not yet come! Worrying of wolves,
Biting of mad dogs, the manges and the –

Enter DOG [*now white*]

---

6 *Tomalin* Diminutive of Tom; a sign of affection

7 *Revenge ... sweeter* Proverbial (R90)

8 *raven* As a bird of ill omen. Mother Sawyer's greater powers of understanding
and speech may be inconsistent with her position but this allows the playwrights
to make her more sympathetic and to underscore some issues in the play

10 *fire ... ice* Struggling for forceful language, Mother Sawyer has only outmoded
Petrarchisms

18 *bulch* bulchin or bullcalf; a term of endearment

19 *swart* black

DOG
How now! Whom art thou cursing?
SAWYER
Thee. Ha! No, 'tis my black cur I am cursing,
For not attending on me.
DOG   I am that cur.   30
SAWYER
Thou liest. Hence, come not nigh me.
DOG   Bow, wow.
SAWYER
Why dost thou thus appear to me in white,
As if thou wert the ghost of my dear love?
DOG
I am dogged, list not to tell thee, yet
To torment thee. My whiteness puts thee   35
In mind of thy winding sheet.
SAWYER   Am I near death?
DOG
Yes, if the Dog of Hell be near thee. When
The Devil comes to thee as a lamb,
Have at thy throat.
SAWYER   Off, cur.
DOG   He has the back
Of a sheep, but the belly of an otter: 40
Devours by sea and land. Why am I in white?
Didst thou not pray to me?
SAWYER
Yes, thou dissembling hell-hound.
Why now in white more than at other times?

29–75 (Q is printed in prose)

31 *nigh* near

32 *Why ... white* Goodcole writes, '*Question. In what shape would the Diuell come vnto you? Answere. Alwayes in the shape of a dogge, and of two collars, sometimes of blacke and sometimes of white*' (sig. C2v). According to his account of *Daemonologie* in 1621, Edward Fairfax's daughter Helen saw supernatural agents in the forms of a black cat and a white cat

34 *dogged* perverse, cruel. Dog's trick on Mother Sawyer (by turning white) is the last act of victimization against her in the play

36 *winding sheet* shroud
     sheet (sweet Q)

39 *Have at* guard

41–2 *Why ... me?* So Goodcole: '*Would the Diuell come vnto you, all in one bignesse? Answ. No; when hee came vnto mee in the blacke shape, he then was biggest, and in the white least; and when that I was praying, hee then would come vnto me in the white colour*' (sig. D1v)

DOG
    Be blasted with the news; whiteness is day's foot-boy,   45
    A fore-runner to light, which shows thy old rivelled face.
    Villains are stripped naked, the witch must be beaten
    Out of her cockpit.
SAWYER   Must she? She
    Shall not; thou art a lying spirit.
    Why to mine eyes art thou a flag   50
    Of truce? I am at peace with none;
    'Tis the black colour or none, which I fight under.
    I do not like thy puritan paleness.
    Glowing furnaces are far more hot
    Than they which flame outright. If thou
    My old dog art, go and bite   55
    Such as I shall set thee on.
DOG   I will not.
SAWYER
    I'll sell my self to twenty thousands fiends,
    To have thee torn in pieces then.
DOG   Thou canst not.
    Thou art so ripe to fall into hell, that no more   60
    Of my kennel will so much as bark at him
    That hangs thee.
SAWYER   I shall run mad.
DOG   Do so.
    Thy time is come to curse, and rave, and die.
    The glass of thy sins is full, and it must run out at gallows.
SAWYER
    It cannot, ugly cuz, I'll confess nothing;   65
    And not confessing, who dare come and swear
    I have bewitched them? I'll not confess one mouthful.

45 *foot-boy* page
46 *rivelled* wrinkled
48 *cockpit* A place for cockfights, a common sport, with a pun on the Cockpit
    Theatre where this play was performed in London
53 *puritan* hypocritical
59 *torn in pieces* Cf. II.i.136
64 *glass* hourglass
    run out (of time)
65 *I'll confess nothing* Confessions were not taken on oath since they were self-
    incriminating. This gives more point and purpose to chaplains like Henry
    Goodcole for their services (and, in his case, publications)

DOG
  Choose, and be hanged or burned.
SAWYER
  Spite of the Devil and thee, I'll muzzle up
  My tongue from telling tales.   70
DOG
  Spite of thee and the Devil, thou'lt be condemned.
SAWYER
  Yes, when?
DOG   And ere the executioner catch thee
  Full in's claws, thou'lt confess all.
SAWYER
  Out dog!
DOG   Out witch! Thy trial is at hand.
  Our prey being had, the Devil does laughing stand.   75

          The DOG *stands aloof. Enter* OLD BANKS, RATCLIFFE
                    and COUNTRYMEN

OLD BANKS
  She's here; attach her. Witch, you must go with us.
SAWYER
  Whither? to hell?
OLD BANKS
  No, no, no, old crone; your mittimus shall be made thither,
  but your own jailors shall receive you. Away with her.

          [*They take hold of* MOTHER SAWYER]

SAWYER
  My Tommy! My sweet Tom-boy! O thou dog!   80
  Dost thou now fly to thy kennel and forsake me?
  Plagues and consumptions –

                              Exeunt [*all except* DOG]

DOG   Ha, ha, ha, ha!
  Let not the world, witches or devils condemn,

---

  68 *hanged or burned* One popular belief was that witches who confessed would
      have the lesser punishment of hanging; in fact, only witches found guilty of mur-
      dering their husbands or masters were burned
  76 *attach* arrest
  78 *mittimus* A warrant ordering a person to be imprisoned until trial
  81 *Dost ... me?* Thus Goodcole: 'being descried, to pay in the ende such a worker
      of Iniquity, her wages, and that which shee had deserued, (namely, *shame* and
      Death) from which the Diuell, that had so long deluded her, did not come as shee
      said, to shew the least helpe of his vnto her to deliuer her: but being descried in
      his waies, and workes, immediately he fled' (sig. A4v)

They follow us, and then we follow them.

[*Enter*] YOUNG BANKS *to the* DOG

YOUNG BANKS

I would fain meet with mine ingle once more; he has had a   85
claw amongst 'em. My rival, that loved my wench, is like to
be hanged like an innocent; a kind cur where he takes; but
where he takes not, a dogged rascal. I know the villain loves
me.

[DOG] *barks*

No! Art thou there? That's Tom's voice, but 'tis not he; this   90
is a dog of another hair. This? Bark and not speak to me?
Not Tom then. There's as much difference betwixt Tom
and this, as betwixt white and black.

DOG

Hast thou forgot me?

[DOG *barks*]

YOUNG BANKS

That's Tom again. Prithee ningle speak, is thy name Tom?   95

DOG

Whilst I served my old Dame Sawyer, 'twas. I'm gone
From her now.

YOUNG BANKS

Gone? Away with the witch then too. She'll never thrive if
thou leavest her; she knows no more how to kill a cow, or
a horse, or a sow, without thee, than she does to kill a   100
goose.

DOG

No, she has done killing now, but must be killed
For what she has done. She's shortly to be hanged.

YOUNG BANKS

Is she? In my conscience if she be, 'tis thou hast brought her
to the gallows, Tom.   105

DOG

Right. I served her to that purpose, 'twas part of my wages.

---

85 *fain* willingly, gladly

85–6 *he ... claw* Naive Young Banks has no difficulty in recognizing the work of
the Devil

87 *innocent* (1) guiltless; (2) idiot

98 prefix *YOUNG BANKS* (DOG Q)

101 *goose* (1) idiot; (2) prostitute. Contemporary authors were arguing that as servants of the Devil, witches made no decisions on their own

106 *DOG* (sig. H4 in Q which misnumbers p. 55 and p. 35)

YOUNG BANKS

This was no honest servant's part, by your leave Tom. This
remember, I pray you, between you and I; I entertained you
ever as a dog, not as a Devil.

DOG

True; and so I used thee doggedly,　　　　　　　　　110
Not devilishly. I have deluded thee
For sport to laugh at. The wench thou seekst
After thou never spakst with, but a spirit
In her form, habit and likeness. Ha, ha!

YOUNG BANKS

I do not then wonder at the change of your garments, if you　115
can enter into shapes of women too.

DOG

Any shape to blind such silly eyes
As thine; but chiefly those coarse creatures,
Dog or cat, hare, ferret, frog, toad.

YOUNG BANKS

Louse or flea?　　　　　　　　　　　　　　　　120

DOG

Any poor vermin.

YOUNG BANKS

It seems you Devils have poor thin souls, that you can
bestow yourselves in such small bodies. But pray you, Tom,
one question at parting (I think I shall never see you more)
where do you borrow those bodies that are none of your　125
own? The garment-shape you may hire at broker's.

DOG

Why wouldst thou know that? Fool,
It avails thee not.

YOUNG BANKS

Only for my mind's sake, Tom, and to tell some of my
friends.　　　　　　　　　　　　　　　　　　130

DOG

I'll thus much tell thee. Thou never art so distant
From an evil spirit, but that thy oaths,
Curses and blasphemies pull him to thine elbow.
Thou never tellst a lie, but that a Devil
Is within hearing it; thy evil purposes　　　　　135
Are ever haunted; but when they come to act,

---

110 *doggedly* affectionately, in contrast to Dog's low opinion of Young Banks at
　　lines 117–18

126 *broker's* pawnbroker's, second-hand dealer's

131–40 *Thou … thee* Since the Devil's agent is giving conventional Puritan doctrine
　　here, the speech is both polemical and satirical

As thy tongue slandering, bearing false witness,
Thy hand stabbing, stealing, cosening, cheating,
He's then within thee. Thou playst, he bets upon thy part;
Although thou lose, yet he will gain by thee.   140

YOUNG BANKS
Ay? Then he comes in the shape of a rook.

DOG
The old cadaver of some self-strangled wretch
We sometimes borrow, and appear human.
The carcass of some disease-slain strumpet,
We varnish fresh, and wear as her first beauty.   145
Didst never hear? if not, it has been done.
An hot luxurious lecher in his twines,
When he has thought to clip his dalliance,
There has provided been for his embrace
A fine hot flaming Devil in her place.   150

YOUNG BANKS
Yes, I am partly a witness to this, but I never could embrace
her. I thank thee for that, Tom; well, again I thank thee,
Tom, for all this counsel; without a fee too. There's few
lawyers of thy mind now. Certainly Tom, I begin to pity
thee.   155

DOG
Pity me? For what?

YOUNG BANKS
Were it not possible for thee to become an honest dog yet?
'Tis a base life that you lead, Tom, to serve witches, to kill
innocent children, to kill harmless cattle, to 'stroy corn and
fruit, etc. 'Twere better yet to be a butcher, and kill for   160
yourself.

DOG
Why? These are all my delights, my pleasures, fool.

YOUNG BANKS
Or Tom, if you could give your mind to ducking, I know
you can swim, fetch and carry, some shop-keeper in
London would take great delight in you, and be a tender   165

---

141 *rook* (1) a black bird; (2) a swindler
147 *twines* embraces
148 *When ... dalliance* when the Devil embraces the lecher
159 *'stroy* destroy
160 *etc.* (& Q) Hoy conjectures & to be 'a sign that the actor is to go on speaking
     extemporaneously' (III, 266)
163–5 *ducking ... delight* The use of water spaniels for duck hunting was a popular
     sport

master over you. Or if you have a mind to the game, either
at bull or bear, I think I could prefer you to Moll Cutpurse.

DOG

Ha, ha! I should kill all the game, bulls, bears, dogs,
And all, not a cub to be left.

YOUNG BANKS

You could do, Tom, but you must play fair, you should be   170
staved off else. Or if your stomach did better like to serve
in some nobleman's, knight's, or gentleman's kitchen, if
you could brook the wheel, and turn the spit, your labour
could not be much; when they have roast meat, that's but
once or twice in the week at most, here you might lick your   175
own toes very well. Or if you could translate yourself into
a lady's arming puppy, there you might lick sweet lips, and
do many pretty offices; but to creep under an old witch's
coats, and suck like a great puppy, fie upon't! I have heard
beastly things of you, Tom.   180

DOG

Ha, ha! The worse thou heardst of me, the better 'tis.
Shall I serve thee, fool, at the self-same rate?

YOUNG BANKS

No, I'll see thee hanged, thou shalt be damned first; I know
thy qualities too well, I'll give no suck to such whelps;
therefore henceforth I defy thee; out and avaunt.   185

DOG

Nor will I serve for such a silly soul.
I am for greatness now, corrupted greatness;
There I'll shug in, and get a noble countenance.
Serve some Briarean footcloth-strider,

167 *bull or bear* the sports of bull-baiting or bear-baiting
   prefer recommend
   Moll Cutpurse Mary Frith, a well-known woman in London who dressed in
   men's clothing and had a reputation as a fighter, a bawd and a cutpurse; this may
   be a self-referential joke since Dekker had improved her reputation in his play
   about her, *The Roaring Girl* (1611), written with Thomas Middleton
171 *staved* driven or beaten; a term used for dogs in bull- and bear-baiting
173 *wheel* treadwheel (that turned a spit in roasting)
177 *arming puppy* a small dog carried in the arms
178 *offices* services
185 *out and avaunt* be off with you
186 s.d. *DOG* (sig. I1 Q; p. 57 misnumbered here as p. 41)
188 *shug* elbow, force the way, shove
   countenance patronage
189 *Briarean footcloth-strider* corrupt official; (Briareus was a giant in Greek
   mythology who had 100 hands; an ornamented footcloth indicated high rank)

That has an hundred hands to catch at bribes,   190
But not a finger's nail of charity.
Such, like the dragon's tail, shall pull down hundreds
To drop and sink with him. I'll stretch myself,
And draw this bulk small as a silver wire,
Enter at the least pore tobacco fume   195
Can make a breach for. Hence silly fool,
I scorn to prey on such an atom soul.

YOUNG BANKS

Come out, come out, you cur; I will beat thee out of the
bounds of Edmonton, and tomorrow we go in procession,
and after thou shalt never come in again. If thou goest to   200
London, I'll make thee go about by Tyburn, stealing in by
Thieving Lane. If thou canst rub thy shoulder against a
lawyer's gown, as thou passest by Westminster Hall, do; if
not, to the stairs amongst the bandogs, take water, and the
Devil go with thee.   205

Exeunt [YOUNG] BANKS, DOG *barking*

Act V, Scene ii

Enter JUSTICE, SIR ARTHUR [CLARINGTON], WARBECK,
[SOMERTON, OLD] CARTER [*and*] KATHERINE

JUSTICE

Sir Arthur, though the bench hath mildly
Censured your errors, yet you have indeed

---

192 *dragon's tail* As a common image of punishment; see Rev. 12:3–4
197 *atom* tiny, irrelevant
199 *procession* The 'beating of the bounds', a formal periodic establishment of
    boundaries reinforced through a perambulation of them
201 *Tyburn* The chief London location for public executions
202 *Thieving Lane* A short street in Westminster curving from the west side of King
    Street to Broken Cross, the route thieves were taken to Gatehouse Prison; cf.
    Rowley, *Match at Midnight*, I.i; sig. C2
203 *Westminster Hall* A court of justice along the Thames west of London
204 *stairs* landing-place on the Thames
    bandogs mastiffs used to guard the steps
    take water embark

0 s.d. *Enter ... KATHERINE* (Q does not designate new scene)
1 *bench* (1) judge; (2) court

Been the instrument that wrought all
Their misfortunes. I would wish you paid down
Your fine speedily and willingly.

SIR ARTHUR   I'll need no urging to it.   5

OLD CARTER

If you should 'twere a shame to you; for if I should speak
my conscience, you are worthier to be hanged of the two,
all things considered; and now make what you can of it.
But I am glad these gentlemen are freed.

WARBECK

We knew our innocence.

SOMERTON   And therefore feared it not.   10

KATHERINE

But I am glad that I have you safe.

Noise within

JUSTICE   How now! What noise
          is that?

OLD CARTER

Young Frank is going the wrong way. Alas, poor youth!
Now I begin to pity him.

                                        [*Exeunt*]

Act V, Scene iii

Enter YOUNG [FRANK] THORNEY *and Halberds. Enter
as to see the Execution,* OLD CARTER, OLD THORNEY,
          KATHERINE, WINIFRED *weeping*

OLD THORNEY

Here let our sorrows wait him. To press nearer
The place of his sad death, some apprehensions
May tempt our grief too much, at height already.
Daughter, be comforted.

---

12 *the wrong way* to the gallows (for a misdirected life); cf. the proverb for some-
     thing going amiss (W168)

0   s.d. *Enter ... weeping* (Q does not designate new scene)
     Halberds Soldiers who carried halberds, spears with an axe-blade at the head
1   *wait him* Old Thorney suggests Frank is not on stage; perhaps the stage direc-
     tion refers to his passing over the stage, with guards
4   *Daughter* daughter-in-law

WINIFRED   Comfort and I
Are too far separated to be joined   5
But in eternity. I share too much
Of him that's going thither.

OLD CARTER
Poor woman, 'twas not thy fault. I grieve to see thee weep
for him that hath my pity too.

WINIFRED
My fault was lust, my punishment was shame;   10
Yet I am happy that my soul is free
Both from consent, foreknowledge and intent
Of any murder. But of mine own honour,
Restored again by a fair satisfaction,
And since not to be wounded.

OLD THORNEY   Daughter, grieve not   15
For what necessity forceth; rather resolve
To conquer it with patience.
Alas, she faints!

WINIFRED   My griefs are strong upon me.
My weakness scarce can bear them.

[VOICES] within
Away with her! Hang her, Witch!   20

Enter [MOTHER] SAWYER to execution, OFFICERS with
halberds, [and] COUNTRY-PEOPLE

OLD CARTER
The witch, that instrument of mischief! Did not she witch
the Devil into my son-in-law, when he killed my poor
daughter? Do you hear, Mother Sawyer?

SAWYER
What would you have? Cannot a poor old woman

---

13 *But* and
14 *satisfaction* repentance, atonement
15–16 *grieve ... forceth* 'Never grieve for what you cannot help' was proverbial
(G453)
20 *Hang ... Witch!* Although witchcraft was taken seriously under King James,
only 35 executions are recorded between 1603 and 1616 and only five between
1616 and 1625, including Mother Sawyer's
s.d. *Enter ... COUNTRY-PEOPLE* 'On Saturday, being the fourteenth day of
Aprill, *Anno Dom.* 1621. this *Elizabeth Sawyer* late of *Edmonton*, in the County
of *Middlesex* Spinster, was arraigned, and indited three seuerall times at Iustice
Hall in the Old Baily in *London*' (Goodcole, sig. B1v)
24–5 *What ... vexation?* 'Thus God did wonderfully ouertake her in her owne
wickednesse, to make her tongue to be the meanes of her owne destruction'
(Goodcole, sig. B1)

Have your leave to die without vexation?   25

OLD CARTER
Did you not bewitch Frank to kill his wife? He could never
have done't without the Devil.

SAWYER
Who doubts it? But is every devil mine?
Would I had one now whom I might command
To tear you all in pieces. Tom would have done't   30
Before he left me.

OLD CARTER
Thou didst bewitch Anne Ratcliffe to kill herself.

SAWYER
Churl, thou liest; I never did her hurt.
Would you were all as near your ends as I am,
That gave evidence against me for it.   35

FIRST COUNTRYMAN
I'll be sworn, Master Carter, she bewitched Gammer
Washbowl's sow, to cast her pigs a day before she would
have farrowed, yet they were sent up to London, and sold
for as good Westminster dog-pigs, at Bartholomew Fair, as
ever great-bellied ale-wife longed for.   40

SAWYER
These dogs will mad me. I was well resolved
To die in my repentance; though 'tis true,
I would live longer if I might. Yet since
I cannot, pray torment me not; my conscience

26 *bewitch Frank* Mother Sawyer has no involvement in Susan's death; Old Carter's
    accusation is another instance of village victimization
32 *Thou ... herself* Cf. Goodcole: '*Question. Whether did you procure the death of
    Agnes Ratcliefe, for which you were found guilty by the Iury? Answere.* No, I
    did not by any means procure against her the least hurt' (sig. C2v)
37 *cast* give birth to
39 *dog-pigs* Male roasted pigs, a common item of sale at Bartholomew Fair in
    Smithfields, London (on St Bartholomew's Day, 24 August)
40 *great-bellied ale-wife* Common belief held that pregnant women especially
    craved roast pig
41 *dogs* cowards
42–5 *though ... be* Thus Goodcole: '*Quest. What moues you now to make this con-
    fession: did any vrge you to it, or bid you doe it, is it for any hope of life you doe
    it? Answ.* No: I doe it to cleere my conscience, and now hauing done it, I am the
    more quiet, and the better prepared, and willing thereby to suffer death; for I
    haue no hope at all of my life, although I must confesse, I would liue longer if I
    might' (sig. D1v)

Is settled as it shall be. All take heed   45
How they believe the Devil; at last he'll cheat you.
OLD CARTER
Thou'dst best confess all truly.
SAWYER   Yet again?
Have I scarce breath enough to say my prayers?
And would you force me to spend that in bawling?
Bear witness, I repent all former evil;   50
There is no damned conjuror like the Devil.
ALL
Away with her, away!

                    [*Exeunt* MOTHER SAWYER *with* OFFICERS]

          Enter FRANK *to execution,* OFFICERS, JUSTICE, SIR
          ARTHUR [CLARINGTON], WARBECK [*and*] SOMERTON

OLD THORNEY
Here's the sad object which I yet must meet
With hope of comfort, if a repentant end
Make him more happy than misfortune would   55
Suffer him here to be.
FRANK   Good sirs, turn from me;
You will revive affliction almost killed
With my continual sorrow.
OLD THORNEY   O Frank, Frank!
Would I had sunk in mine own wants, or died
But one bare minute ere thy fault was acted.   60
FRANK
To look upon your sorrows executes me
Before my execution.
WINIFRED   Let me pray you, sir.
FRANK
Thou much wronged woman, I must sigh for thee,
As he that's only loath to leave the world,
For that he leaves thee in it unprovided,   65
Unfriended; and for me to beg a pity
From any man to thee when I am gone,
Is more than I can hope; nor to say truth,
Have I deserved it. But there is payment

45–6 *All . . . you* Mother Sawyer's contrition and her death as a warning to others
    anticipates Frank's death (cf. 73–90) where both deliver the play's moral mes-
    sage, but her early and more abrasive remarks (33–5) complicate any easy judg-
    ment of her

58 *O Frank, Frank!* (italics Q)

Belongs to goodness from the great exchequer   70
Above; it will not fail thee, Winifred;
Be that thy comfort.
OLD THORNEY   Let it be thine too,
  Untimely-lost young man.
FRANK   He is not lost,
  Who bears his peace within him. Had I spun
  My web of life out at full length, and dreamed   75
  Away my many years in lusts, in surfeits,
  Murders of reputations, gallant sins
  Commended or approved; then though I had
  Died easily, as great and rich men do,
  Upon my own bed, not compelled by justice,   80
  You might have mourned for me indeed; my miseries
  Had been as everlasting, as remedyless.
  But now the law hath not arraigned, condemned
  With greater rigour my unhappy fact,
  Than I myself have every little sin   85
  My memory can reckon from my childhood.
  A court hath been kept here, where I am found
  Guilty; the difference is, my impartial judge
  Is much more gracious than my faults
  Are monstrous to be named; yet they are monstrous.   90
OLD THORNEY
  Here's comfort in this penitence.
WINIFRED   It speaks
  How truly you are reconciled, and quickens
  My dying comfort, that was near expiring
  With my last breath. Now this repentance makes thee
  As white as innocence; and my first sin with thee,   95
  Since which I knew none like it, by my sorrow,
  Is clearly cancelled. Might our souls together
  Climb to the height of their eternity,
  And there enjoy what earth denied us, happiness.
  But since I must survive, and be the monument   100
  Of thy loved memory, I will preserve it

---

70 *great exchequer* dispensation in heaven (the great exchequer is God)

77 *Murders* (sig. I2v; Q misnumbers p. 60 as p. 43)

84 *fact* crime, evil; this is a common term in contemporary pamphlets for alleged acts of witchcraft

87 *court* Presumably the quarter sessions of assizes which judged all major criminal cases bound over to it by the local court; the playwrights have collapsed the time to parallel the judgments on Mother Sawyer, which was routine and swift, with that of Frank, which would have been referred

With a religious care, and pay thy ashes
A widow's duty, calling that end best,
Which, though it stain the name, makes the soul blest.

FRANK
Give me thy hand, poor woman; do not weep.   105

[*They hold hands*]

Farewell. Thou dost forgive me?
WINIFRED   'Tis my part
To use that language.
FRANK   Oh that my example
Might teach the world hereafter what a curse
Hangs on their heads, who rather choose to marry
A goodly portion, than a dower of virtues!   110
Are you there, gentlemen? There is not one
Amongst you whom I have not wronged: you most;
I robbed you of a daughter; but she is
In heaven; and I must suffer for it willingly.

OLD CARTER
Ay, ay, she's in heaven, and I am glad to see thee so well   115
prepared to follow her. I forgive thee with all my heart; if
thou hadst not had ill counsel, thou wouldst not have done
as thou didst. The more shame for them.

SOMERTON
Spare your excuse to me, I do conceive
What you would speak. I would you could as easily   120
Make satisfaction to the law, as to my wrongs.
I am sorry for you.
WARBECK   And so am I.
And heartily forgive you.
KATHERINE   I will pray for you,
For her sake, who I am sure, did love you dearly.

SIR ARTHUR
Let us part friendly too. I am ashamed   125
Of my part in thy wrongs.
FRANK   You are all merciful,
And send me to my grave in peace. Sir Arthur,
Heavens send you a new heart. [*Turns to* OLD THORNEY]
   Lastly to you, sir;
And though I have deserved not to be called

---

115 *Ay, ay* (sig. I3; Q misnumbers p. 61 as p. 44); Q prints this speech as poetry

Your son, yet give me leave upon my knees,   130
To beg a blessing.

[FRANK *kneels*]

OLD THORNEY   Take it. Let me wet
Thy cheeks with the last tears my griefs have left me.
O Frank, Frank, Frank!
FRANK   Let me beseech you, gentlemen,
To comfort my old father, keep him with ye;
Love this distressed widow; and as often   135
As you remember what a graceless man
I was, remember likewise that these are
Both free, both worthy of a better fate,
Than such a son or husband as I have been.
All help me with your prayers. On, on, 'tis just   140
That law should purge the guilt of blood and lust.

Exit [with OFFICERS]

OLD CARTER
Go thy ways. I did not think to have shed one tear for thee,
but thou hast made me water my plants spite of my heart.
Master Thorney, cheer up, man; whilst I can stand by you,
you shall not want help to keep you from falling. We have 145
lost our children both on's the wrong way, but we cannot
help it. Better or worse, 'tis now as 'tis.
OLD THORNEY
I thank you sir; you are more kind than I
Have cause to hope or look for.
OLD CARTER
Master Somerton, is Kate yours or no?   150
SOMERTON
We are agreed.
KATHERINE   And, but my faith is passed,
I should fear to be married, husbands are
So cruelly unkind. Excuse me that
I am thus troubled.
SOMERTON   Thou shalt have no cause.
JUSTICE
Take comfort, Mistress Winifred. Sir Arthur,   155
For his abuse to you, and to your husband,

---

133 *O ... Frank!* (italics Q)
143 *water my plants* weep
146 *on's* of us
155–8 *Take ... marks* (Q assigns this speech to [Old] Cart[er])

Is by the bench enjoined to pay you down
A thousand marks.

SIR ARTHUR   Which I will soon discharge.

WINIFRED

Sir, 'tis too great a sum to be employed
Upon my funeral.   160

OLD CARTER

Come, come, if ill luck had served, Sir Arthur, and every
man had his due, somebody might have tottered ere this,
without paying fines. Like it as you list. Come to me,
Winifred, shalt be welcome. Make much of her, Kate, I
charge you. I do not think but she's a good wench, and hath   165
had wrong as well as we. So let's every man home to
Edmonton with heavy hearts, yet as merry as we can,
though not as we would.

JUSTICE

Join friends in sorrow; make of all the best.
Harms past may be lamented, not redressed.   170

                                        Exeunt

Epilogue

WINIFRED

I am a widow still, and must not sort
A second choice, without a good report;

158 *marks* coins worth 13s.4d. each, or two-thirds of a pound sterling; this fine is
   comparatively a very large one
   soon discharge Sir Arthur's ready willingness to pay, and his ability next to
   Mother Sawyer's poverty and Old Thorney's potential bankruptcy, pointedly
   and ruefully displays the privilege of class and underscores Frank's mixture of
   guilt (for murdering Susan) and innocence (of Sir Arthur's manipulation of him)
159 *too great a sum* Winifred's line confirms the play's concern with class distinctions as permanent as well as privileged, and as unassociated with morality and
   intention
162 *tottered* swinging, as in being hanged
163 *Like ... list* whether you like it or not
   Come to me Old Carter's invitation further condemns Sir Arthur
166–70 *So ... redressed* The troubling and unsettled ending of the play is not so
   much a structural weakness as a fairly common convention for tragicomedy and
   here a true reflection as well of the troubling and complicated characters and
   social situations as yet not fully resolved

1 *sort* make

Which though some widows find, and few deserve,
Yet I dare not presume, but will not swerve
From modest hopes. All noble tongues are free;   5
The gentle may speak one kind word for me.

PHEN.

Finis.

7 *PHEN.* Ezekiel Fenn, the actor, identified by Bentley (II, 433) as a boy born in
the parish of St Martin in the Fields in 1620. He played Sophonsiba in Nabbes'
Hannibal and Scipio, presented at the Cockpit in Drury Lane in 1635 by Queen
Henrietta's Company, as well as Winifred in this play. Henry Glapthorne's
Poems (1639) has a 'Prologue' written 'For *Ezekial Fen* at his first Acting a
Man's Part'